Making Love Work *while* Leading Your Family

MARRIAGE LESSONS FROM A POWER COUPLE

DRS. SAMUEL, JR., & ANDREA

HAYES

Foreword by Dr. John P. Kelly

Ⓟ *Pensiero Press*

Making Love Work While Leading Your Family:
Marriage Lessons from a Power Couple

Pensiero Press

Websites: www.ThePensieroPress.com | www.LentzLeadership.com
Twitter: https://twitter.com/drcheryllentz
Facebook: https://www.facebook.com/Dr.Cheryl.Lentz

Books are available through Pensiero Press at special discounts for bulk purchases for the purpose of sales promotion, seminar attendance, or educational purposes.

Volume ISBN: 978-1-7329382-8-1

*Kindle and electronic versions available

Cover design & production: Gary Rosenberg
www.thebookcouple.com

CONTENTS

TESTIMONIALS

"Doctors Samuel and Andrea Hayes, a young couple with a Godly vision for today's young people. Equipped with extensive natural experience, business skills, and a spiritual conscience, they have constructed a masterpiece that should be read by all pastors and spiritual leaders of today. This work will and can be an excellent helping tool in any ministry. My part in their journey was small, but I consider myself privileged and blessed for God to have allowed our paths to meet. May God continue to bless and anoint your lives in the wisdom and knowledge of His Word."

> —Bishop Dr. Allen Malone, Founder and President of Ministerial Alliance Association of the Apostolic Faith, Inc., Pastor of Bethlehem Holy Ghost Headquarters Church, AZ

"U.S. Army Major Sam Hayes is a brilliant military strategist who has learned many valuable life lessons that can aid all of us who are married. His biblical perspective will prove applicable for various relational dynamics for generations to come!"

> —Bishop Dr. Joseph Mattera, Convener of the U.S. Coalition of Apostolic Leaders, Founding Pastor of Resurrection Church, NY

"This book is a valuable resource for the Body of Christ. It provides insight for married couples to understand that a marriage is established on God's plan for our lives. The marital relationship mirrors our relationship with Christ. The leadership insights are crafted thoughtfully which should allow couples to reflect and to develop strategies to improve areas in the marriage that are challenges. This book will benefit couples in building stronger marital relationships in the Kingdom."

—Rev. Dr. Peggy L. Owens and Rev. Ray P. Owens, Sr., Pastor, Franklin Chapel African Methodist Episcopal Zion Church, NC

First, we give honor to our Lord and Savior, Jesus Christ without whom none of this would be possible. We would like to dedicate this book to our children (Stefone, Shirod, and Ashara) because they are the reason that we strive to go the extra mile. To our parents (Albert and Rosie Marsh; Samuel and Marcia Hayes), thank you for being there to support us even when we did not believe in ourselves. To our brothers (Albert Jr., Shawn, and Sheldon) thank you for all of your support. To Bishop Dr. Allen Malone and Mother Martha Malone, thank you for bridging the gap while we were away from our parents, to Apostle Dr. James McGrady Jr., who developed us and Apostle Kim and Pastor John Balthrop, who placed us in our destiny. To Apostle Dr. John P. Kelly, who launched us to the nations, thank you for playing a vital role in our development. To all of our mentors within the AME Zion Church, thank you for being there to guide us. We would also like to thank everyone who has poured into our lives. We love you all and thank God for you.

FOREWORD

Marriage is under attack from many external sources, but the greatest and most harmful attack comes from within the marriage dynamic itself. I have said many times, "The greatest enemy to my success or achievement in any area of my life is me." In other words, what can destroy a marriage or generate a divorce comes down to you or your spouse.

Many think the most terrible and base things in life such as addictions of alcohol, drugs, pornography, verbal, physical, emotional abuse, infidelity, economics, the death of a child are severe problems and the main reasons for divorce. These are severe problems that result in terrible and often irreconcilable behavior to a spouse, to a child, children, or other family members.

Severe problems are extremely volatile and emotional issues that cause severe emotional reactions and often lead to the dissolution of marriage and resultant divorce. These are terrible things, but they are not statistically the most common reason for divorce. So, what is the major reason for divorce?

Researchers tell us that only 14% of divorces are the result of severe problems, many of which I stated above. Therefore, 86% of divorces are primarily caused by non-severe problems. How can that be?

People have desires for love, for intimacy, for expectations, and goals, often without effective tools to share life together.

This can create more heat than light and more emotional reactions than loving thoughts and solutions to cover each other and build together.

We have internal emotional reactions to numerous issues one encounters in marriage and leading a family. So, what is the most important issue in making love work while leading your family? How does a husband and wife do that? By having and displaying emotional maturity!

This means stop and think, take a deep breath, so you don't emotionally react but act rationally. Discuss the art of love, discover the art of making decisions as a couple.

As you read Dr. Samuel, Jr., and Dr. Andrea Hayes' book, *Making Love Work While Leading Your Family*, you will discover the secret art of creating a successful loving marriage and fulfilling family.

This book is their love gift to you, your marriage, and family. It is a must read!

Dr. John P. Kelly
International Convenor for International Coalition
of Apostolic Leaders

About the Foreword Author . . .

Dr. John P. Kelly is distinguished as an anointed master builder and master strategist by leaders in business and ministry throughout the world. His experiences as an educator, bridge builder, businessman, athlete, and minister have prepared him to train and inspire hundreds of thousands of people to achieve their destiny.

He is the Founder and International Convening Apostle of International Coalition of Apostolic Leaders (ICAL) and President of John P. Kelly Ministries, Inc. His books and seminars address the strategies and actions needed to advance the Kingdom of God. **www.johnpkelly.org / www.icaleaders.com**

PREFACE

After 20 plus years of marriage and many ups and downs, we wanted to acknowledge our journey. The experiences that we've had throughout our marriage helped us develop the unconditional love that we have for each other and influenced how we lead our family. It is our desire to share some of those experiences and insights with others in the hopes of helping to strengthen other marriages.

Understanding the significance of hard work in a marriage is essential to maintaining a marriage that is healthy and lasting. Throughout the book, we emphasize the key elements that help promote healthy communication and the ability to relate to each other in an impactful way. We also focus on the significance of not only having a strong marriage, but helping couples effectively lead their families and be an example for their children and others who may admire them.

As we worked to develop the book, it was a very reflective experience. The challenges that we have overcome were emphasized, and it helped us appreciate our journey and each other even more. It reminded us that marriage is not easy, and it takes commitment and *staying power* to make it work. The ability to reflect on challenges and victories that we have experienced in our marriage helped us to realize our purpose together, giving us more momentum to continue on the journey together.

As a power couple, it was difficult. Over the years, Samuel served and continues to serve as soldier. Through the ranks of an enlisted member and officer, he was often away from home. Whether for year-long unaccompanied assignments, 15-month long or short 6-month deployments, various training exercises in and outside the country, or the many schools needed for his career progression; he was gone a great deal.

Andrea had to pick up the slack in not only running the home but also advancing her career. While Samuel was gone defending the country, she continued to raise our three wonderful kids, maintaining a home that was full of love and peace, in an effort to resemble some sense of normalcy. Andrea was not only the glue for the kids, but also Samuel's link to the kids, hopes, dreams, and fears. Beyond challenges of home, she advanced from a school teacher to a counselor, creating a safe environment for kids to learn and grow. Andrea focused her passion on helping her students and clients have a voice that matters.

When Samuel was home, they remained active in the church. From member to church leader, Samuel advanced through the spiritual ranks—layperson, minister, and youth minister, elder, prophet, and apostle—and grew in his gifting. Andrea did as well; she expanded her ability to minister in song, in preaching the Word of God, and in the prophetic. Together, we not only matured in the house of the Lord, but also impacted our churches, fellowships, and communities for the better.

We also impacted our communities in other ways. Andrea uplifts her surroundings as a member of Delta Sigma Theta Sorority, Inc. She takes part in community service events in the local community and within her church. Samuel also enhances his community as a member of Kappa Alpha Psi Fraternity,

Inc. He strives to build and mentor young men into productive members of communities while at home and abroad. We are committed to community service and actively work in the church, making it better for the new generation of leaders.

Andrea's aspiration inspires Samuel. Her lifelong dream of earning a PhD motivated him to follow her lead. Her goal challenged them, since they were courting in college and now, 20 years later, it has become a reality—Dr. Samuel, Jr. and Dr. Andrea Hayes. Both of us transitioned into life-long learners, based on becoming our best selves. With our hard-earned degrees, we contribute to our fields through growing multiple businesses focused on impacting our communities in which we live and love.

It is through these challenges—staying together, raising a family, serving in the military, growing in God, impacting the community, serving in the church, and building multiple businesses—that we distill our experiences into lessons learned. We use our life to illustrate examples of the good, the bad, and the ugly. We also describe how the Word of God assisted us through the ebbs and flows of marriage. Additionally, we have included scripture as a source of connection with God's Word and His will for marriage. The vital points are framed in thought provoking questions, for each partner, group, or bible study discussion. While reading this book, we encourage our readers to embrace the interactive structure of the book. Ultimately, we want to be a resource available for you and the organizations you serve to improve God's institution of marriage.

ACKNOWLEDGMENTS

As with our journey and the things we have accomplished in our lives, this book would not have been possible without the love and support of many.

We would not be who we are today without the great examples from our parents. Andrea's parents modeled for us how to grow older gracefully with each other in their golden years, while investing in their children and grandchildren. Samuel's parents showed us how to break barriers, establishing new standards of marriage excellence for generations to come. Together with this solid foundation, we are positioned not only to advance our family, but also the next generation of married couples.

Amidst this global pandemic, there is absolutely no way that we could have completed this book without the help of each other and our children. Samuel was deployed in Turkey for a year unaccompanied tour, while Andrea was home leading on the home front. Our kids unknowingly provided continued motivation. Together with love, we forged an uncharted path with this being our first book and taking care our family during this difficult time.

Our editor, Dr. Cheryl Lentz, was our guidepost, making the journey easy. Cheryl's enthusiasm and passion drew us to her. She has a wealth of knowledge and experience that made implementing our vision for the book look easy; thank you. We would also like to extend a thank-you to her talented team, specifically Gary Rosenberg, an exceptional graphic designer who captured the spirit of the book in art form, and media partner Rebecca Hall-Gruyter, who helped launch this book into the marketplace.

Finally, we want to thank every person we ever encountered during our marriage. To all the individuals and couples who gave us encouraging words and healing hugs—to those who helped our marriage grow through the difficult moments by crying and listening; we thank you for being you.

CHAPTER 1.

YOUR SPOUSE IS NOT YOU: UNREALISTIC EXPECTATIONS

Early in our marriage, we really did not understand each other. In many cases, we had unrealistic expectations. Our uninformed thoughts are not unique to us because many couples had similar experiences. Unfortunately, divorce rates, as illustrated across the globe: (a) 38% in Canada, (b) 44% in Germany, (c) 46% in North America, (d) 51% in Russia, (e) 55% in France, and (f) 65% in Spain ("Divorce Rate by Country," 2020) are unsettling at best. The lack of success indicates, however, that there is problem with understanding what is necessary and required for a successful marriage. Like these individuals, we struggled to find our way. Regardless of those who had irreconcilable differences or found success, we offer our approach that may help those who are struggling too.

Early in our marriage, we really did not understand each other. In many cases, we had unrealistic expectations.

We followed God's plan, learning some critical lessons along the way. Our experience was harder than it should have been. Early on in our marriage, we experienced life then turned to God, eventually we got wiser and followed His plan step-by-step. As we reviewed what should have happened, we learned some things. From our early marriage experiences, this chapter focuses on our problems with different viewpoints, miscommunication, and money, highlighting our lessons from marriage and leadership enabling us to grow into a stronger couple.

Upbringing

Our upbringing shaped us, informing our thoughts on marriage. Although we grew up similarly regarding our faith, we had differences within our background and experiences. Regardless of our individual threads, we were able to bring them together and weave our lives in a way that makes a unique tapestry, illustrating a diverse, multitalented, and beautiful family that loves God. Designed within our family's garment is our roots, our present, and our dreams of the future. Exploring the details of our lives will give the context to our lessons.

Samuel's roots were shaped by the U.S. military. His family moved around internationally (Panama and Germany) and within the United States (Florida, Alaska, and North Carolina). Samuel's family developed a lifestyle from moving every 3 years on average. His good experiences included seeing the world, fueling Samuel's desire to travel and learn about different cultures; his bad experiences included leaving close friends before he was ready, enabling him to have intense friendship, but detach quickly from people and move on like nothing happened. Samuel was a product of a U.S. Army family, as a military brat, who became a soldier himself.

His view of the world, before marriage, was hopeful and idealistic. With his parents having him at a young age of 17 years old; they not only spent a lot time with Samuel, but also gave him a youthful outlook of the world, framed by God's Word. Samuel's exposure abroad in different countries and cultures enabled him to understand many different points of view. When he saw a gulf between people's understanding, Samuel tried to bridge the misunderstanding between them. Inherently, he saw the good in people and gave them the benefit of the doubt. Samuel was successful in life—sports, school, and business—but regardless of his various successes, he still dealt with the fear of failure. Samuel's determination would help him battle his insecurities. His hard-earned life perspective became his blueprint, which he hoped to share with Andrea. Ultimately, Samuel strived to improve this guide with his family, providing them with a generational roadmap for life.

By contrast, Andrea was raised in a traditional household. Although her father served in the U.S. military, he separated years before she was born. While born in Florida, the biggest move for her family was from Florida to North Carolina when she was 7 years old. Following that move, Andrea moved twice more within an hour from each location. The transition was not very difficult because there was family very close by and time with extended family was a priority that provided a phenomenal level of stability. This predictability afforded her the ability to anchor in a community, thereby enhancing her school and church.

Growing up in a Christian household, she was taught values and the importance of having integrity and strong morals. Her

parents had her around their mid-thirties and were very sup-
portive of her, encouraging her to strive to reach her goals and
work hard to accomplish them by doing her best at whatever
she decided to do. The motivation that her parents instilled in
her helped influence the drive to achieve with excellence.

Comparing the experiences between our upbringing, illuminated connections and friction points. We had some similarities
to include (a) a foundation with Christ and (b) a drive to want
more out of life, which made it easier to grow together. On the
contrary, we had more differences that include (a) the experiences of a military family moving a lot compared to traditional
families staying in one city, (b) our parents had different perspectives based on starting their families with Samuel's parents
being young and figuring out life together compared to Andrea's
parents' stability being older and more prepared for parenting,
and (c) a different outlook on marriage roles. Unknowingly, we
had more differences than similarities, which made the journey
more difficult yet sweeter.

Our families' upbringings influenced us differently, especially
regarding what marriage should and should not be. Differences
that we brought to the relationship clashed, affecting us significantly in the beginning of our marriage. Some of the differences
impacted us in a good way and others in a not so good way.
For example, the closeness with Andrea's family influenced
the lack of desire for Andrea to seek extensive friendships outside of her family unit which fostered an appearance of being
unapproachable to others. Through various experiences and
interactions with Samuel, Andrea began to view relationships
differently. Andrea's change is one example of many, resulting
in her challenging herself to become better. The point is that
we had to do the hard work, identifying places where we could

improve ourselves as a team and individually, learning how to work together in a new way.

Differences that we brought to the relationship clashed, affecting us significantly in the beginning of our marriage.

It was a challenge, although we learned how to compromise with each other. We had to do away with the unrealistic expectations and remember that we were two determined and stubborn individuals from different backgrounds. Instead of us trying to defend our differences, over time; we built bridges. These bridges were at first made of straw and stick, and then they became stronger, eventually being made of brick and mortar. Ultimately, the glue that held us together were our similarities as we began to court each other.

Dating

We started dating in college at Fayetteville State University in Fayetteville, North Carolina. Beyond meeting through a close friend (Andrea's best friend and Sam's prayer partner), we were attracted to each other. We were drawn to each other's youthful looks and our similar dreams. Andrea is gorgeous; a tall drink of water, with goals of earning a PhD impacting the world, inspiring all in her circle of friends and family. Samuel was a determined, hard-working business owner selling his clothing line, Samuel Hayes Clothing, out of the trunk of his car with goals of running a global company someday. However, we knew there was something more, something deeper, yet unknown at the time. As we began to learn more about each other, we recognized that we constantly stumbled over differences in how we would go about doing things as well as how we each would approach important topics. These clashes were difficult to overcome at first; we eventually did in time.

As we went on dates, we quickly discovered that eating a meal was complicated. Samuel's background embedded in him that sharing was not only normal, but also desired. He was the oldest child and grandchild (on his Jamaican mother's side) and his role was often to look out for others, which usually required sharing what they had with those in need. Conversely, he was one of the youngest grandchildren on his father's side, interacting with his older cousins and observing his father's love for family enhanced Samuel's commitment to maintain a close bond with relatives. This quality led Samuel to want to share his food on dates or ask to taste Andrea's food. This was met with resistance from her because she did not grow up with the same openness.

Andrea's background was a little different from Samuel's. Although dinner was eaten together and significant time was spent together as a family, when it came to food, you ate what was on your own plate. She remembers vivid examples of Samuel ordering something opposite of what she did. She would become upset, wondering why he did not order what she ordered, if he wanted to taste it. With the differences of opinions, there was constant conflict between Samuel and Andrea surrounding this issue. Underneath the sharing or not sharing concept were embedded certain values of community and individual, which clashed beyond the idea of sharing food in our relationship.

Throughout dating, we saw similarities and differences. Unknowingly dating provided a roadmap of the good, the bad, and the ugly. For example, in exploring our different views of sharing food, our challenges with solving problems and communicating issues were illuminated. For one of us, not having a daily itemized plan for the vacation may be a problem or not having a budget may be a problem for the other. We realized retrospectively that this map showed us the areas that we must not only challenge our own ideas about certain topics, but also negotiate with each other to find our way in our marriage that works for us. The food example is only one of the many we experienced while dating, even though it is full of lessons and insights. Next, we turn to another important phase of our life.

Unknowingly dating provided a roadmap
of the good, the bad, and the ugly.

The Beginning of Marriage

Seeds exposed in our dating continued to grow. The seed of miscommunication was the byproduct from not addressing our different viewpoints. Not only did a lack of communication cause chaos in our relationship, consequently miscommunication also weakened the relationship between family and friends. For instance, one of us would seek guidance from our extended support group on what we thought was going on between us, yet the attempt only complicated matters. Our support group would then give us advice on unknowingly wrong information, which often made the situation worse. We learned not only to truly understand what the other person meant by their actions, but also to limit the help received from our respective outside support groups. Although friends and family have great intentions, we recognized we needed to mature and solve our own problems without making others a part of our personal conflicts.

Becoming one was difficult and required us to grow up. We did not want to let go of who we thought we were. However, we tried to build bridges of trust to allow us to grow together. Interestingly, our identities were still based on our parents' and friends' ideas of who we were and not how we saw each other. As the challenge continued to evolve, we became better as a couple and not perceived as something less than what we were before. For example, becoming husband and wife, as defined by God, was our goal. We learned not to focus on what others thought our marriage should be because what made us happy was the most important. Lessons from our parents could inform us, and even show us, however, not define us. The truth of the matter is that both our parents are still married and have successful marriages. This lesson was difficult because we valued our family and friends' opinions, yet we realized that each generation does things a little differently and each relationship is different. We had to find our own way. Make no mistake, finding our way meant trial and error, hurt and pain, as well as success and failure, but at the end of the day, our experiences and our truth made us better.

We did not want to let go of who we thought we were.

Another area, in particular, in which we did not agree when we were first married was money. How were we going to approach our finances? This question was not only important, it was the source of many arguments. Samuel wanted to combine all of our funds in one bank account and Andrea desired to have some funds together and some separate. Over time, we came to a compromise. Once we became more financially stable, we decided to budget an agreed upon amount per month for our individual use. Such an agreement aided with us honoring each other's thoughts, resulting in a tailored approach for us rather than following the many examples from our friends and family.

At the beginning of our marriage, we had challenges understanding how to handle our finances. Samuel was a Private First Class (E-3), in the U.S. Army, overseas stationed in Korea. Andrea was a college student who worked and focused on caring for our young son. We did not have much money, compounded by each having different ideas on how to spend it. In the midst of this financial learning curve, we were raising our first child, who was 1 year old at the time. We learned a similar lesson here; although, our friends and families had success with their money, our differences were in our goals. These results helped determined what was best for us as a Christian and military family with businesses. Eventually, our approach met our goals and overcame the lack of funds through sacrifices and savings, resulting in financial resilience.

One of the hardest challenges came from a period of no income for 4 months when Samuel was a Specialist (E-4). When Samuel returned from Korea, we packed up and moved our new family to Arizona. As Samuel in-processed into his new unit, he discovered that his signing bonus was paid twice, and the U.S. Army wanted the money back, all at once. Thus, he received no money for the next 4 months. Interestingly enough, Samuel's father, on active duty during the time, advised Samuel to put the extra money away just in case the U.S. Army requested their money back. Samuel listened, but over time he began spending it. Little was left when the U.S. Army or sometimes called *Uncle Sam* recognized the discrepancy concerning Samuel's overpayment.

Talk about bad timing! We had our new family in a new location solely dependent on Samuel's income to make it, nevertheless God's blessings prevailed. No matter how big or small our income, we believed in and practiced tithing which meant giving 10% of our income to God. To aid with the lack of funds, Samuel secured an emergency loan from his unit. Together, we cut back and made our funds last. As funds ran low, Andrea went to the mailbox and received an unexpected check from our car insurance agency that claimed we were over charged, and this was a refund. Talk about being right on time! This money was more than enough to cover the remaining needs until Samuel's next paycheck. We both praised God for His blessings and His mercies. Consequently, this hardship brought us closer together. We made it on our own without any help from our support groups, which proved to be to our benefit in the long run; learning how to make it with just us and God.

Our Problems and God's Answers

Our problems needed attention; we needed help, so we turned to the Lord. We sought direction and guidance from the scripture. It was through His Words that we found not only hope, but also a way to think about our problems and process them from a different perspective, eternally. The Apostle Paul informed us from his context, and we chose these lessons to apply to our marriage. Paul's words of wisdom, insight, and encouragement shifted our mindsets from us and our problems to the maker, God, and His purpose for us. Shifting our minds to Him saved us from ourselves and turned our problems into opportunities to glorify Him.

It was through His Words that we found not only hope, but also a way to think about our problems and process them from a different perspective, eternally.

Problems with different viewpoints. Different viewpoints caused us not to appreciate each other and view the other person's thoughts, words, and deeds that were different in a degrading manner. This was not right; we found hope in the scriptures. Romans 12:3-5 helped us with acknowledging that every part supplies the whole. Paul's words were aimed at the believers in Rome to transform them into a powerhouse among one of the greatest civilizations in the ancient world. Paul's concept was important for us to understand because of assisting us with seeing the good in each other rather than just the differences. These words also aided us with seeing a new beginning, when we came together as one, which resembled becoming a power-house for God, as Paul suggested. However, we almost missed it because of our focus on the negative instead of the positive.

Our opposing views also helped us to humble ourselves to each other. We both were stubborn and bullheaded, yet Paul reminded us not to think more of ourselves than we ought to think. Paul was speaking about humility in relationship to one's peers and God. Paul's words challenged our past. We were not considerate of what the other felt or said; however, we had to let our egos go and deal with each other with love and a sound mind. For example, through love, we were able to see clearer what each other tried to say rather than a perceived negative action. This humility approach was not always easy, yet when applied, it proved to be invaluable.

Our opposing views also helped us to humble ourselves to each other.

Problems with miscommunication. Different viewpoints left unclarified, often led to miscommunication, which caused us to sometimes assume the worst, rather than understand the truth. Reading God's Word challenged us to find the truth. Romans 12:6-21 showed us how to address honoring each other. Interestingly, Paul addressed the issues of different spiritual gifts and their operation. Also, Paul was addressing how to behave like a Christian. Both strategies directly addressed miscommunication between coworkers for Christ and neighbors in the community of which Paul's recommendations resulted in the idea for us to treat each other as a friend versus a foe. The idea of honoring each other in thoughts, words, and deeds took on a different perspective as we placed each other in a new place of royalty as king and queen.

Another aspect of Paul's concept meant for the Romans, assisted us with loving God first and understanding that He would draw us closer together. Paul spoke about the Lord who fights our battles while emphasizing that we should not take it into our own hands. For the Christians in Rome, this was very real, as they were dying for their faith. Although we were not dying physically, at times, the love was dying between us. Paul's words hit home. Sometimes, we performed acts of kindness towards each other, even when we were mad, because God was watching, and His Word prevailed. In time, we saw that the seeds of love that were being planted blossomed and healed the pain between us.

Sometimes we performed acts of kindness towards each other, even when we were made, because God was watching, and His Word prevailed.

Problems with money. Money problems were complicated by not listening to ourselves. Our miscommunication was amplified with us trying to implement the good ideas from others before we truly understood how we wanted to operate; our routine was not properly defined. Romans 14:1-21 helped us focus on ourselves versus worrying about family and friends. Paul's message to the Romans addressed the gray areas of life, relationships, and motives. It was from these gray areas of listening to one's convictions and finding our way that we learned how to find our voice concerning money. Through trial and error, we were able to chart a path of our own and not one dictated by family and friends. In this new territory, we gained an appreciation for each other by bonding through hardships and celebrating successes. We even better understood the advice from others, because we had our system firmly in place and talked about it before we implemented their advice. We were a team.

Another aspect of Paul's lessons to the Romans that helped us with money was when he addressed the complex issue of eating meat versus vegetables. Paul's lessons espoused acting in love towards each other regardless of differences. From this lesson, we applied love to our differences with money—one account versus two separate accounts. In time, we grew our one account to many that we both have access to, but we also budgeted certain amount of money that we used for our purposes. If we exhausted the budgeted funds, we had a certain amount we could spend from our joint accounts without prior discussion. However, if the item goes over the agreed amount then we would review our budget and have a discussion before either of us made the purchase. This system enables us to have transparency and trust. Paul addressed the difference in food related to observing the law, as we transitioned different views in money systems to a happy household.

Marriage Lessons

From our experiences with dating and the beginning of our marriage, as well as the Word of God, we learned many lessons. One of the most important lessons came from a counseling session with Bishop Dr. Allen Malone. We sought his guidance because we wanted to give up on our marriage. As our pastor in Arizona, he simply asked us why? Beyond describing the symptoms of what we perceived to be the problem and associated feelings, we really did not know why. Yet, we were tired of feeling angry, disappointed, and upset with each other and did not see any way out but, the "D" word. To this day, we vowed to never say that word to each other.

Yet, we were tired of feeling angry, disappointed, and upset with each other and did not see any way out but, the "D" word.

Ultimately, each of our responses did not clearly answer Bishop Malone's question. After he patiently waited through our failed attempts, he explained what we were going through. Bishop stated that we were experiencing growing pains which offered a starting point for healing. We were married young, in our early twenties, with a young son. Bishop further explained that we truly did not know ourselves, let alone how to interact with each other. Bishop's sage wisdom enabled us to slow down and learn from each other, instead of thinking we should know what the other was feeling or what was meant by our actions. Bishop's guidance took the pressure off us, but he left the "D" decision up to us.

After reflecting on this counseling session, we agreed to slow down, try to understand each other better, and not assume what the other meant. It was difficult and painful, but we were committed to doing the hard work. Interestingly, we wanted to give up, but reflectively, we realized that we did not give up at the same time which could have been a big problem, if we did. This slower pace of patiently dealing with conflict in our marriage allowed us to focus on the issues and not the person. Looking around at our family, we took inventory. The fact that we had a child who depended on us, provided us with the motivation to keep going.

Marriage lessons on different viewpoints. Becoming one is hard. It takes constant effort to blend one's life with your spouse. Together, you both can see more, process more, and accomplish more. Do not be afraid to work together to achieve what you want in life. Andrea always says, "Teamwork makes the dream work."

Marriage lessons on miscommunication. Advice from others outside of your marriage, can be viewed as miscommunication. Don't assume that the advice received from outside sources is what is best for you and your relationship. Although the advice may be coming from loved ones, it doesn't mean that it is always right because they are not a part of your relationship. What works for them, may not work for you and your spouse.

Marriage lessons on money. Determine your path together and be up front—separate accounts or one account, hidden account for a rainy day or an account together. Have the difficult conversations. Getting different perspectives is great, but together, you and your spouse should determine what is best for *your* family.

These lessons are ours, yet we know that some couples may disagree. Our different viewpoint on the lessons, for example, may be challenged by couples who are married but operate separately. If you decide to operate individually within your marriage, we encourage you to consider how not being united, concerning finances, may cause isolation leading to a lack of trust. Those who choose to listen to outsiders' experiences for guidance in their marriage have to be careful of good intentions, but potentially wrong advice for them. Such advice may not work for their marriage and could cause more harm. Last, dealing with money is a huge part of being married; our lessons are for team players. Whether you are a team or not, some couples may decide that our approach is not for them and go forward in a different way. However, we offer that if your way is not agreed upon, then seeds of distrust may grow into conflict later; please be careful.

In short, it is important for you and your spouse to come to a mutual agreement and honor your decision. The ability to be on one accord not only helps strengthen your marriage, but it shows those who look up to you what it means to be unified and gives them a living example of a strong marriage. Sometimes it is difficult to agree, but if there is mutual respect for one another, compromise comes much easier, especially as you learn from God's leadership.

Leadership Insights

We learned much from our marriage and God's leadership. His plan for marriage showed us how much we did not know. We should have espoused to some of God's principles as a husband should love, lead, and provide for his family (Eph. 5:25-29; 1 Cor. 11:3; 1 Tim. 5:8) and as a wife should help, manage, and love her family (Gen. 2:18, 21-22; 1 Tim. 5:14; Titus 2:4), but at times, it was hard. Even though we were familiar with ideas on marriage as an institution, the difficult part was truly applying His framework to our lives.

However, we saw the plan in the Word.

However, we saw the plan in the Word. Genesis 2:24 stated, "This is why a man leaves his father and mother and becomes attached to his wife, and they become one flesh." To be honest, we did not know the work required to make this happen, which we detailed to offer insight. Over time, we recognized there was a formula for success coded in the statement and follows as:

- *A Man*—indicates maturity
- *Leaves*—transitions
- *Father and Mother*—model of a complete family
- *Attached*—a new family
- *His Wife*—complement

17

- *They Become*—a process of learning, friendship, and trust
- *One Flesh*—deep intimacy between two people

Accomplishing the implied actions in the above insights is a big challenge, however, they are necessary for success the way God designed. If a boy leaves home before he matures into a man, for example, the lack of maturity could cause problems and major damage in the relationship. Conversely, if a wife does not complement her husband, then they both could be competing on the battlefield of life and marriage unnecessarily. From the problems outlined in our marriage, there are many lessons such as marriage and leadership. Now, we share with you our leadership insights gained from the problems described in this chapter, as an attempt to pay it forward to the next generation of married couples.

Leadership insights on different viewpoints. Just as becoming one is hard, leading your family is harder. Ensuring that an environment is created where the both of you can grow and mature is essential. This space needs to be a safe environment not only to grow as an individual, but also as a couple. From this lens, the desired teamwork is in view.

Creating an environment for growth can be simple or hard; this depends on the couple. Having the right mindset is key to establishing a safe environment, especially in your home. Another key to growth could be using a safe word that creates a moment to deal with matters of the heart. When processing what the other's heart is saying, these actions of—respecting, understanding, not judging, listening, and hearing—are a few that may help with achieving teamwork.

Leadership insights on miscommunication. Understanding what works for others may not work for you is key. Therefore, design how the two of you want to communicate, while addressing the fact that men and women think, perceive, and respond differently. Men speak what they are thinking, and women speak what they are feeling, so becoming in tune with each other requires listening.

The key to communication is understanding which requires listening. Failure to listen contributes to communication problems, which can be avoided. As Andrea says, "We have two ears, two eyes, and one month; listen and watch twice as much as you speak." Her statement implies giving someone your full attention, which helps towards really listening and becoming a better communicator.

Leadership insights on money. Husbands create the environment to have the difficult conversation about finances. This action directly relates to your wife growing. As she grows, conversations can be had about views on managing resources. Understand what tools and systems are required for your family to be successful and ensure essential needs are met.

As described before, creating a safe environment is not only vital to establishing a team mentality, but also critical towards stewardship. Being on one accord and applying God's stewardship principle in Genesis 1:28, results in dominion. In turn for being faithful over a little, God will entrust us with more.

Being on one accord and applying God's stewardship principle in Genesis 1:28, results in dominion.

Some couples may not subscribe to our insights, which are inherently grounded in scripture. Alternate views and approaches may work out fine, however, we focused on our faith in God. Such other perspectives may include addressing different viewpoints, miscommunication, and money from as self-centered perspective as compared to a team approach. The idea of the lone ranger or the superhero may be romantic in the beginning, but in the long run, this notion may become exhausting for the person who saves the day. This action may also sow seeds of resentment that can become friction points later in the marriage.

Therefore, it is important for you and your spouse to know that God's plan works. The difficult part is applying His plan to your marriage. However, following His blueprint provides a path to success; we learned this the hard way by doing our own thing. Just as we grew to learn to submit our wills to God and trust Him with our lives, we learned that God looks after us. As Andrea says, "He looks after fools and babies," with that said, we are no longer babies.

Conclusion

In this chapter we have tried to show that unrealistic expectations can occur with your spouse. From our illustration of our different upbringings, our dating, and our marriage, we distilled how important recognizing opportunities to blend the various experiences versus allowing them to become friction points within a marriage. With our eyes toward identifying opportunities compared to problems, we learned God can answer our problems with His Word.

With our eyes toward identifying opportunities compared to problems, we learned God can answer our problems with His Word.

God provided the needed answer(s) to our prayers. He gave us marriage lessons and leadership insights. Our marriage lessons had us searching for mutual agreement by coming together as one after leaving the comfort of our parents' home to build a home for our family. God's leadership insights showed us that the environment in our home is critical to develop not only a space to mature, but also as a space to strengthen a bond together. Such a bond will be needed in Chapter 2, as we discuss overcoming divorce. Below are some thought provoking questions to help you think about your relationship as it relates to God's plan. Last, if an individual or a couple wants to have the resolve in Christ as we did, turn to the appendix for the salvation prayer.

QUESTIONS FOR REFLECTION
AND DISCUSSION

1. **Different viewpoints**—How do you identify, discuss, and come to an understanding of different viewpoints? How do you create the environment to discuss different points? How are you willing to embrace the viewpoints of your spouse without being judgmental?

2. **Miscommunication**—What is your objective when you seek advice from others outside of your marriage? What do you intend to gain? How are you willing to protect the agreements made between you and your spouse regardless of outsiders' opinions?

3. **Money**—What feelings do you attach to money? If there is a difference of opinion on finances, what compromises are you willing to make? If you were to write a 5-year financial plan, what would it be?

CHAPTER 2.

KNOW THE VALUE OF YOUR SPOUSE: AVOIDING THE PITFALL OF DIVORCE

Understanding how valuable your spouse is when it comes to what each of you adds to the relationship is very important. Valuing your spouse is critical when it comes to making your partner feel appreciated. Unfortunately, some couples do not even make it to marriage because they are not confident in their ability to overcome divorce. For instance, according to the U.S. Census Bureau (2020), from 2008 to 2018, the national marriage and divorce rates showed a decline. Although these statistics may look promising considering a decline in both areas, we encourage you to consider that the decline in divorce is likely a direct reflection of the decline in marriages overall. Some couples are not comfortable enough to enter into a marriage, while some others continue to have a hard time with finding the sweet spot in marriage. Similar to these couples, we struggled to find our way and had to fight for each other.

Along the way, we found strength in God as we fought for our marriage. From our foxhole, we learned that we had to fight back-to-back against the world. Interestingly, this conflict not only allowed us to find ourselves, but also made us stronger. We gained strength from our combat experiences. Chapter 2 focuses on our problems with value, faith, love, and respect, demonstrating our lessons gained throughout our struggles showing our newfound strength as a couple focused on God's promises.

Deployments

Well before the fighting, God intervened and validated our marriage. Only a few months into dating, God spoke through Andrea and confirmed the extent of our union. It was destined for this marriage to take place. Beyond the Word received from the Lord, Samuel asked for confirmation and received it in three different ways from thoughts to food to prayers; God answered each request within moments. Although Samuel made sure he heard from God, his naive testing became a faith-building block. Samuel's resolve was cemented in the Lord's confirmation, which unknowingly proved to be critical later, as an ambush was being prepared.

Throughout our marriage, Samuel was away from home in foreign countries for approximately 60 months, with over 20 months in combat. The most difficult deployment was the first one, which was 15 months in Iraq. Beyond Samuel being in harm's way, the separation was difficult for many reasons. For example, Andrea had the sole responsibility of maintaining the household and her career, while keeping her sanity together. We were lucky to be semi-together for 2 years before Samuel deployed because of field training and disaster relief. We were within the first 5 years of marriage with three young kids under the age of 10 years old, as he prepared to leave for Iraq.

The most difficult deployment was the first one, which was 15 months in Iraq.

During this time, Andrea began her career in the education field. She was a young teacher who loved making a difference with the children she taught. For her, seeing young students have light bulb moments were some of her greatest joys. In addition, Andrea thoroughly enjoyed helping students find their voice and express themselves in ways that mattered to them and the world. She transitioned from elementary to middle school education, earning teacher of the year along the way. Andrea blossomed into a role model that students would follow over the course of her career, providing a guidepost for students struggling to find their way.

Samuel advanced as an officer, leading soldiers into combat. He transitioned from the rank of Staff Sergeant (E-6) to the rank of 2nd Lieutenant (O-1E), after graduating Officer Candidate School (OCS). He received a scout platoon in his first unit. Although, Samuel was *home* the first couple of years, he wasn't really there. Samuel was always preparing for combat. He was constantly gone, as in going to survival and leadership schools, helping the victims of Hurricane Katrina, training for combat, and deploying to Iraq. As we got our minds ready for his deployment, we realized that Samuel's new position required more of him and less time for us and our family. With competing priorities, our past ambushed us. Samuel's soldiers were ready; our marriage was not.

Our marriage under attack. Relationships from the past ambushed our marriage. Unresolved connections produced doubt about the future, contributing to confusion. For instance, we both became affected by past relationships from a first love to a best friend. These effects caused uncertainty in the back of our minds as we both prepared for the deployment. Samuel focused on the war zone; Andrea concentrated on the home front. Samuel often stated that Andrea had the harder job between them, although he was in a combat zone in Iraq. From our minds to deep in our hearts, confusion, doubt, and fear became the center of attention as we said, "see you later." Andrea does not believe in saying goodbye. Amid the separation, a war broke out for our love. This war challenged us beyond our breaking points. These obstacles were thoughts about our marriage, the influence of past relationships, and having dual careers while raising a family. Although God ordained this marriage, there were times where neither of us wanted to hear that. We were done!

Amid the separation, a war broke out for our love.

As mentioned in Chapter 1, we were contemplating the big "D," but God had other plans for us. As noted in the scripture, what God has joined together, let no man put asunder (Matt. 19:6; Mark 10:9). Even though the Word of God supported us, making our marriage work was difficult; as they say. "the struggle was real." There were times in our marriage when we did not want to look at each other, we fought every day, and even faced some situations that tested every aspect of our relationship and staying power. We allowed things from the past to resurface, which almost tore us a part. Our ability to overcome these challenges was embedded in each other's value. Obstacles we dealt with were misunderstandings, confusion, blame, and shame; frequently, these roadblocks were aimed at each other, instead of at solving the problem. Once we recognized that the seeds of success relied on truly understanding what each other brought to the table, then things began to turn around in our marriage.

Andrea's fight (in her voice). As a new wife entering a marriage with a *ready-made* family, it was a struggle. Not only did we raise our oldest son, we raised each other. In addition, we welcomed another son and a daughter. I have often heard others say that there is not an instruction manual for raising children; the same goes for marriage.

Samuel and I are two very head-strong people and we had our share of disagreements. One of the sources of our arguments was the principle of a wife honoring her husband as the head of the household. As a young wife, I did not want to *submit* to my husband. For instance, my mother always showed me an example of how to treat my husband. I should cook his dinner, fix his plate, and put it on the table for him. I didn't want to do that. Half of the time, I didn't even like my husband (to be honest).

Pushing through the discomfort, I fought hard for my marriage.

Pushing through the discomfort, I fought hard for my marriage. While Samuel deployed, I dealt with a relationship from the past, resulting in a focus on the future rather than the past.

Being challenged was painful, as I needed time to heal from the confusion in my mind. Not only was this journey necessary to becoming a better woman, wife, and mother, this transition also made me stronger. The lessons of letting go of the past allowed me the ability to enjoy the present and create the future.

Balancing family and career by myself was not the plan. I not only ensured the house was maintained to the best of my ability, but I also had to provide the kids with a sense of normalcy, such as allowing them to play in youth sports leagues, go to church, and stay connected with Samuel. Running the house was complicated by itself, and I was also committed to my new career. While wearing my *superwoman cape*, I established myself as a teacher with promise. I was consumed with work and the kids' activities daily; sometimes I did not know how we survived, but we did!

As we grew together and experienced more challenges than both of us can count, in time, I learned the importance of honoring my husband as the head of the household. I learned the value of cooking for him, making his plate, and putting it on the table. When I truly understood the impact of being a Proverbs 31 woman, my husband began to treat me like his queen. I noticed that he started to compliment me more, the way he started looking at me was more endearing, and he became more willing to do things to make me happy.

Sam's fight (in his voice). As a young husband and father, I struggled to lead my family. With young children and a new wife, we had different expectations of our roles. For example, we came from different backgrounds that provided different opinions. Therefore, our ideas of marriage conflicted and made building from the same mental model difficult, thereby not setting a good foundation for our family. Providing for them and protecting them was my top priority; however, I had to find my way to accomplish that for my family.

I was in warfare on many fronts. My heart fought for my marriage, while my body was in combat. I struggled with the battle in my heart, because I did not want my wife to struggle with anything, yet several time zones separated us. For instance, I could not protect her from growing pains, as she dealt with a past relationship, took care of our family, and launched her career. Although hurtful, I realized she became stronger as a woman, mother, and wife. Seeing Andrea transform encouraged me in my faith and my marriage.

My heart fought for my marriage, while my body was in combat.

As the war raged in Iraq, I witnessed the power of God in our marriage. I was strengthened while facing a determined enemy. This fight was fierce. I was shot at and my vehicle was blown up. Unfortunately, many soldiers lost their lives. Yet, God saved me. While fighting, I focused on my soldiers, myself, and God's children. Not only was I praying for others, but I was also preaching once a month at a U.S. base, when our missions completed. Many people became Christians and were baptized. I never forgot that a soldier was killed in an attack the day after giving his life to Christ. In this war-torn place, I reflected on God's promise for my marriage.

After the Iraq war, I fought one more battle at home. Like my wife, I dealt with a past relationship, resulting in increased clarity. With a sense of freedom, I focused on my future and not my past. The act of freeing yourself from dead weight liberates your mind and body from unnecessary stress. God helped me fight through the negative images, thoughts, and feelings in my mind to realize that God put us together. He does not make mistakes. I saw our marriage reach new levels of love and commitment that strengthened our bond. With God's help, I stayed the course for my family.

Our fight (in their voice). Sometimes our flesh is difficult to fight. When one loves another, although they may not be in love, there is an unspoken connection. At the beginning of our marriage, there were many differences. Some of the differences we overcame and some of them we continue to work on. However, in marriage, there has to be constant growth if it is going to work.

As we began to grow together, we recognized more and more that we are two very stubborn, head-strong individuals, and we had to learn to make many compromises. In many instances, we did not want to compromise. Instead, we ignored the other's feelings and devalued each other's opinions. We were emotionally disconnected from each other. The lack of emotional attachment added to the personal attacks, which lead to emotional abuse by hurting each other with our words. This was not fair. When we devalued each other, it made it easier to *throw* the "D" word around because we were not emotionally in tune with each other.

In many instances, we did not want to compromise.

When we realized what was going on, we started to acknowledge that we had to fight. God had too much in store for us and too much work for us to do as a team for us to give up. We had to be an example to our children of what marriage *should* be. We reflected on our marriage and the commitment we made to each other and, most of all, the promise we made to God. We stood before our family and friends and made vows to one another.

As we continued to work diligently to overcome our flesh and began to listen to one another, communication was much easier because we listened to the other person and not just heard what was being said. It must be noted that it took a lot of actively forcing our flesh into subjection by praying, fasting, and crying out before God. The journey was not comfortable. Many times we wanted to give up, but God had another plan. In the end, through all of the struggles, disappointments, and doubts, God still prevailed. The action of mending our hearts brought us closer together. We began to fall in love with one another. We can now say that we are happily married with the love of our lives and would not trade this journey for anyone or anything.

Our Problems and God's Answers

Our problems followed us across time zones, as did God's answers. God provided comfort through His Spirit with specific guidance found in His Word. By reading the scriptures, continuing to pray, and fasting earnestly, we found the solutions to our problems. We heard again from the Apostle Paul, as he spoke to the challenges in our marriage from his ancient pulpit. Paul's words of revelation encouraged us through our hurt and pain, transforming our mindsets from victims of circumstance to victors in Christ Jesus. Changing our minds to a Kingdom perspective was difficult, but very rewarding when we applied His principles to our lives and marriage.

By reading the scriptures, continuing to pray, and fasting earnestly, we found the solutions to our problems.

Problems with value. Not valuing each other caused our love to wane. With our passion decreasing, we lashed out at each other by shaming. Our actions were wrong, and God's Word helped us. Once again, Romans 12:3-5 assisted us with the understanding that every part supplies the whole. With Rome being the center of the ancient world, Paul spoke directly to the Christians at the center of power and influence. Understanding Paul's metaphor of the body was essential for us to see that our success linked us together rather than apart. We neglected each other, for instance, to focus more on each other's careers, family, and friends, creating a void in our marriage. Reflecting on Paul's message allowed us to visualize how life without our spouse would be miserable, as he illustrated with his body metaphor. We saw one as the hand and the other as the foot, either way life would be difficult without each other.

Apostle Paul's words made us reflect! He reminded us to remain humble in Romans 12:3-5, which embodied Jesus's message in Matthew. As noted in Matthew 23:12, "He who exalts himself shall be humbled, and he who humbles himself shall be exalted." In our self-righteous stance, we were selfish. Each of us wanted the other to stop what the other was doing and make the other person the priority. Jesus' message and Paul's words of humility cut to the core of our stubbornness; and it cut deep. They challenged us in our thinking. We were in the marriage together, although we serve different functions that were complementary and not in competition. This value was seen in Andrea's actions of respect and in Samuel's acts of love, which in turn, let us know we were valued by each other.

Problems with faith. Different challenges required different levels of faith. Our problem was that this test was beyond our faith level. Yes we had faith, but our hope in God was tested before in different areas, such as money, cars, and marriage. Romans 1:17 showed us that faith is a building block, which inspired us to grow higher in our faith, like trusting God for the impossible. Paul addressed the Christians in Rome with a statement at the core of his theology; God's grace is open to all that have faith (Rom. 1:17; 3:23). This statement was delivered to an audience unfamiliar with Paul; this principle allowed him to not only communicate what he believed but also, that they were on the journey together. His dual message showed that God has to give us grace in areas that we did not know. For example, in our marriage, God could also be trusted for matters of the heart and beyond our wildest dreams. Paul's recommendations resulted in us growing in our faith, trusting God for the sweet spot in our marriage.

Another aspect of Paul's concept, meant for the Romans, assisted us with growing as individuals. Paul spoke about faith to faith as dimensional, as God's faith inspires man's faith. In his ambassadorial letter to Roman Christians, Paul described the tenets of the faith. Paul also tried to convince them to go with him to Spain. As individuals, we had to trust God for our growth and each other's growth, even though our journey symbolized a roller coaster ride. From our relationship with God, we knew that He would not fail to keep His promises. We had to trust God that everything was going to be alright. As Paul tried to gain support for a future trip, we came together to envision our future together with God.

*As individuals, we had to trust God for our
growth and each other's growth, even though our
journey symbolized a roller coaster ride.*

Problems with love and respect. Love and respect problems were complicated by our hurt and pain, resulting in protecting ourselves and not each other. Focusing inward to self-love rather than outward to love each other was justified by the world's idea of marriage. Such successful marriages seemed to prioritize taking care of self-first over working together as a team, as seen in the increase in pre-marriage agreements. However, Paul offered an alternative perspective in Ephesians. His message delivered from prison, not only addressed the body of Christ through metaphors, but also dealt with leadership at home, which was not about power and control; it was about mutual submission in Ephesians 5:21. From these words, we learned how to let our hearts love through the hurt and the pain. In this space, we valued each other for what we brought to the table rather than what we wanted. We understood how to build towards our future together based on our goals and not others.

Another aspect of Paul's lessons to the Ephesians aided us with our marriage. Ephesians 5:33 helped us with keen insight. Paul wrote: husband love your wife; wife respect your husband. From his lesson, we applied love and respect in a different manner to our marriage. Samuel began to love his wife as Christ loved the church, as he expressed his willingness to die for her. Andrea began to respect her husband as the head of house, praying that God would lead him. As we aligned to God's way and not the world's, we saw a difference in our love. It was deep and became intense. Interestingly through our hard times, we communicated to each other that we could improve in Samuel loving Andrea and Andrea respecting Samuel, which was what God wanted for us, wow! Paul challenged Christians to apply God's ways rather than the prevailing wisdom in ancient times, which proved to be the answer we needed.

Marriage Lessons

From our experiences with being separated by deployments and fighting multiple battles and wars for our marriage, we have learned much specifically from the scriptures. One of the most important lessons came from fighting for our marriage. Yes, facing the conflict was difficult, fighting through our hurt, pain, and disappointment with ourselves and each other was necessary to grow. Standing back-to-back with God's promises in hand, we showed each other that fighting for our marriage was the only option.

Standing back-to-back with God's promises in hand, we showed each other that fighting for our marriage was the only option.

Reflecting on our battle scars, we understood one thing—we could depend on each other! This was the moment we built real trust and true love grew between us. We agreed to listen and try to understand each other's perspectives, along with emphasizing our struggles. For example, what was comfortable for Samuel was not easy for Andrea and vice versa. We had to be patient with each other when the other person operated from a weak area rather than a strong one. Working **with** instead of **against** each other provided us with the opportunity to cover each other's weaknesses, making us stronger.

Marriage lessons on value. Valuing each other is critical to a successful marriage. A fruitful marriage takes continuous work to honor the contributions of each other. Remember, efforts are not in a competition; instead, they are complementary as you work together towards a common goal for you and your family.

Marriage lessons on faith. Trusting God is easier than you think. Sometimes your thoughts and others can confuse your ability to have faith and trust in God. Don't assume that your prayers to God are not heard because it is taking longer than you think it should take. Instead, look at it as an opportunity to get closer to God and build a relationship with Him, which is where the blessings reside.

Marriage lessons on love and respect. Implementing God's marriage plan is better than your plan. A husband needs to love his wife through her love language; so find out what makes her happy. A wife must show her husband respect in a way that he appreciates, to understand his ego. Using a tailor-made approach of love and respect to your spouse paves the way to a God designed marriage.

Some individuals may not agree on how we avoided divorce. Such couples may argue their way is better, which may be true because there is not only one way to have a successful marriage. However, by focusing on other ways that don't involve God, these couples may overlook the deeper problem of the lack of a strong bond among a man, a woman, and God. The bond of three cords demonstrates strength and power making the union difficult to be disrupted.

Therefore, focusing on God, may make it easier for you and your spouse to value each other and avoid divorce. The ability to combat the outside influences, self-doubt, or a lack of faith depends on the relationship between you, your spouse, and God. Strengthening these critical relationships provide a secure refuge that cannot be easily broken because you are on one accord. Being unified in your stance helps prevent divorce.

Leadership Insights

King David illuminated God's leadership in our marriage experiences. In the first book of Samuel, the Prophet Samuel not only saw the rise and fall of King Saul, he saw David fighting for Israel before his death. One of David's battles was at Ziklag, where he fought for the kingdom. As David fought for his family, his men, their families, and others, we saw ourselves in a similar fight for our ourselves, our marriage, our family, and our future. David's fight for his life, which secured his future is detailed in, 1 Samuel 30:1-8:

- Encourage Yourself in the Lord
  - Be convinced before you convince others

- Inquire of the Lord
  - Pursue—get what you go after
  - Overtake—become greater
  - Recover All—that was taken by an enemy

- Full Recovery with a Testimony
  - David was delivered to become a deliverer

King David's fight inspired us to keep fighting! Wow! David sought the Lord and received the answer that was in his favor. Even with David coming from one battle, his loved ones and his men's families were gone. He had to do something, and he did. He went after and pursued them, overpowering them, and recovering all. His leadership pushed beyond a bad situation to seek, pursue, fight, and recover. Just as David, we fought from one battle to the next. From David's leadership, we applied his insights to our problems.

Just as David, we fought from one battle to the next.

Leadership insights on value. The threat of losing a loved one, increases their value. Ensure that your spouse feels valued before anything bad happens. Remember, your spouse is worth fighting for, regardless if they are gone or at home.

Showing value consists of appreciating your spouse for who he / she is as a person. Even in your spouse's absence, making sure they know they are just as important when they are away, helps keep the relationship strong.

Leadership insights on faith. Find your own way to trust God by building your relationship with Him. Looking back over your life, take inventory of what God has done for you. Use these examples as building blocks toward what God can do for you and with you in the future.

The key to building faith is pursing God! Failing to purse Him contributes to a lack of faith and a lack of trust in God's abilities. As Samuel says, from faith-to-faith and glory-to-glory, which is based on the Word. This saying implies that God is building your faith—from an apartment to a house to a mansion. As your faith and trust levels in Him grows, He stretches you, sometimes beyond what you believe.

Leadership insights on love and respect. Recovering all includes God's plan for your house based on love and respect. This action directly involves seeking God and trusting God for wisdom and guidance to flow. Following His plan sows divine seeds that will help with the respect and love you desire to grow.

Building love and respect requires trusting, valuing, compromising, and supporting one another. Being on one accord with God, results in more of God's favor, just like David. This favor can be seen as overcoming in areas where there are challenges or difficulties and, in turn, building your faith in God.

We have drawn strength and encouragement from these insights, but couples may not be convinced. Being certain that teamwork with the Lord's help is better than fighting alone; in our book, it is not a tough sell because we lived it. However, there are some couples who feel that fighting by themselves is a better way. We agree that there are some advantages and disadvantages to fighting alone, however, the point emphasized here is that you can cover more ground as a team. As a true team, we can fight together, knowing that someone has your back.

In sum, fighting alongside each other and not against each other is critical to avoid divorce. The difficult part is that you must keep going from one battle to the next, sometimes fighting alone and as a team. We gained our strength in God and remember that you can too. Embracing your building blocks of faith is easier said than done.

We gained our strength in God and remember that you can too.

Conclusion

The examples, lessons, and insights in this chapter show that knowing the value of your spouse is key to avoiding divorce. We also saw that no battle or war is too hard for God to overcome. Embedded in the examples of us confronting our problems as individuals and as a team, we overcame by our faith in God, but also by working hard and letting go of past relationships. As we kept our minds focused on the future and not the past, we began to apply the lessons and insights that God helped us to find in His Word. We remembered that God's word reminded us in James 2:20, "Faith without words is dead." The works that we put to our faith, through prayer, fasting, and speaking victory over our lives paid off and made our marriage stronger.

In our journey with God, He showed us the lessons and insights we needed to see. God answered our prayers by strengthening us on the battlefields and fighting beside us in our foxholes. Demonstrated through our lessons from marriage, we learned how critical combating outside influences and self-doubt was to build our faith in God and to cement our bond. God's leadership insights showed there is victory in the fight by seeking God, pursing our problems, overcoming our challenges, and recovering our happiness. As we gained faith in God for external challenges, we needed to remember these lessons as we turned inward to work on ourselves individually in Chapter 3 by improving our communication. Below are some questions designed to help with obtaining a mindset for victorious faith.

QUESTIONS FOR REFLECTION
AND DISCUSSION

1. **Valuing each other**—How do you identify your value and communicate it to each other? How do you create an environment to discuss each other's strengths and weaknesses? In what ways are you willing to support your spouse to show that you value them without being critical?

2. **Faith**—What do you expect from God when you seek Him for answers to your problems? How do you build a relationship with Him to strengthen your faith? In what ways are you willing to wait on God to answer your prayers when you are running out of time?

3. **Love and Respect**—What feelings do you attach to love and respect? How do you identify your love and respect language and communicate it to each other? If you were to write a plan on how to love and respect your spouse, what would it be?

Chapter 3.

COMMUNICATION IS KEY: FOCUSING ON THE NON-VERBAL

Communication is often misinterpreted, and non-verbal communication is sometimes overlooked. Conventional wisdom indicates non-verbal communication means to express yourself without speaking to another person or a group of people, such as using the eyes, facial expressions, and gesturing the hands to name a few examples. Surprisingly, research shows that communication, when broken down, equates to approximately 7% verbal and 93% non-verbal (Yaffe, 2011). As married couples, we often underestimate the importance of these gestures and their effect on our marriage. Therefore, understanding your spouse's methods of communication is essential to a healthy marriage.

> *Communication is often misinterpreted, and non-verbal communication is sometimes overlooked.*

In a season of reflection, we focused inward to improve communication within our marriage. What we discovered shocked us. We were becoming petty and bitter as expressed through our microaggressions. From behind our smiles to our frowns, we unknowingly spoke past each other with our expressions. This deep examination ultimately helped us become better communicators. Chapter 3 includes exploration of our problems with identifying non-verbal cues, respecting each other's feelings when communicating, and building effective communication, illustrating that people can improve themselves.

The Unspoken Language

Our period of fighting, as detailed in Chapter 2, was followed by a season of much needed rest. Relaxation and reflection were good for not only us but our entire family. Samuel received orders to move the family to Monterey, CA, where he would graduate from the Naval Postgraduate School (NPS); this school was needed for Samuel's career advancement. Andrea also used this time to study and pass the National Counseling Exam (NCE), enabling her to transition fields from teaching to counseling. Beyond making power moves, we focused on family. This was our family's first time living on the West Coast, so we focused on enjoying each other by traveling and experiencing life. In this space, we began to analyze our marriage for ways to improve, specifically we explored what was behind the unexpressed conflicts.

One of the areas we struggled with was with the unspoken language between us. The truth of the matter was that we addressed our frustrations in non-verbal ways. Surprisingly, neither of us were getting the results we desired, which often made the issues worst. We needed to learn how the other communicated through body language—non-verbal actions. Samuel often tried to determine if he was misinterpreting Andrea's clues and acting on them without really understanding what these clues meant or her intentions behind them. Or Andrea, on the other hand, might have misunderstood what Samuel was trying to communicate by his actions and felt like they were directed at her in a negative manner. Either way, we needed to overcome our miscommunication with each other through our non-verbal assumptions, with finances, as well as attacks on each other to advance our marriage to the next level.

Non-verbal struggle. Over the course of our marriage, we lacked the understanding of how we communicate non-verbally. As a young married couple, we underestimated the significance of non-verbal communication. There were often times we talked past each other and ignored the facial expressions, overt actions, and overall communication with our body language. Yet for the longest time, we did not make communication a priority in our marriage resulting in our marriage suffering because of lack of attention.

As a young married couple, we underestimated the significance of non-verbal communication.

The most obvious means of communication is often verbal because when we speak, it is easier for others to understand our point-of-view. When observing non-verbal communication, it is often misinterpreted, but understanding your spouse's way of communicating on all levels is very important to the development of well-rounded, effective communication.

There is a difference in how we communicate as a couple. Andrea is more of a non-verbal communicator because she often internalizes her feelings. She also tries to work on what these feelings actually mean to her, which increases the level of frustration when her feelings are ignored, either by herself or others. Although Andrea has challenges expressing her feelings verbally, they are expressed through her actions, and sometimes she comes across as aggressive because of built up frustrations. At times, Andrea's suppressed feelings were agitated by Samuel and other times he had nothing to do with what angered her. Either way, when expressing frustrations, sometimes we argued.

Interestingly, Samuel is the opposite of Andrea and that adds to the challenges in communication. He has to *talk* things out **right** away. He is often very vocal about how he feels and what he wants. The struggle comes when those two perspectives *clash*. For example, if Samuel waits for Andrea to process her feelings, he gets anxious and it may cause a problem. Or, if Samuel talks right away, then Andrea may get frustrated. Unfortunately, as we navigate the complexity of marriage, our non-verbal communication goes into overdrive. We began expressing our latent feelings, which not only adds to the confusion, but how we deal with the resulting conflict.

Through our experiences over the years and a plethora of disagreements, we are beginning to learn each other's cues. Samuel is learning to respect Andrea's struggle with verbal communication at times, and Andrea is learning to embrace Samuel's natural ability to be very expressive when it comes to his thoughts and feelings. Although it is a challenge, with love and commitment to one another, we are working hard to overcome most of these challenges to blend our personalities to enhance our marriage. As we move forward, we would like to highlight some examples of specific challenges that we faced and coping mechanisms we used with non-verbal communication and how we continue to work to overcome them in our marriage.

Unspoken challenges with finances. We all know that money is the source of many disagreements in any relationship, let alone marriage. We can recall a specific example in our marriage where we were transitioning from an enlisted family to the family of a military officer. The advancement in Samuel's career and Andrea moving back home to begin her teacher career, helped with the increase in monetary resources. More financial stability made way for Andrea to indulge in something that she loves—shopping.

One of the non-verbal forms of communication for Andrea was shopping, particularly when she was frustrated or upset with Samuel. This non-verbal form of fighting back was not an effective way to handle the frustration because she was spending money without telling Samuel, and he viewed her actions as keeping secrets from him. (By the way, he hates secrets.) The more money Andrea secretly spent, the more Samuel would verbally communicate that her actions in shopping out of emotion upset him. While Andrea was fighting non-verbally, Samuel shared that he felt disrespected which led to more arguments. Samuel began to withdraw, creating more distance in our marriage. We were in a marriage, but in our own *worlds*.

After Andrea reflected on the way Samuel felt, she began to consider his feelings. She started communicating better with him and a compromise was made. Specifically, Samuel shared that he is not opposed to Andrea shopping. In other words, he wanted to be a part of the process, not just an afterthought. For Samuel, this was an opportunity for them to communicate and hopefully talk about why Andrea felt the need to shop, rather than discuss what was causing the problems with him. As a result of being open, we were able to begin to address some of our issues of trust.

Sometimes non-verbal communication is not only misinterpreted but viewed as negative. Gestures, actions, and facial expressions may come across as offensive, but it is very important to understand the source of what is behind the action. Talking to your spouse in times of calm to understand their inner most thoughts may help increase understanding of the non-verbal cues that may be missed otherwise.

Sometimes non-verbal communication is not only misinterpreted but viewed as negative.

Non-verbal attacks during arguments. Withdrawal and isolation are forms of non-verbal attacks we experienced from each other during an argument. As noted, Samuel is very vocal when he is upset or frustrated; Andrea is the opposite. She was always taught that if you don't have anything nice to say, don't say anything at all. Samuel was taught if you have a disagreement, settle the difference quickly so that there is no confusion between the two of you. The difference in approaches often led to clashes, resulting in conflict and, sometimes, non-verbal attacks.

Andrea recognized that she can be very harsh with her words and would try to avoid saying something that she would regret. Therefore, during a disagreement, she often chose silence and that infuriated Samuel, which led to him eventually shutting down. Sometimes Samuel chose to give Andrea a dose of her own medicine to see if she liked similar treatment. After experiencing non-verbal attacks delivered by Samuel during an argument, Andrea felt uncomfortable. The discomfort that she felt when Samuel withdrew caused deep reflection and helped her rethink how she responded to him. Exchanges in perspectives helped us to close the gap between our differences.

Samuel would rarely fight non-verbally; however, when he did, it was primarily through shutting down. He cut off his loving emotion, thoughtful nature, and protective mode. When he would become emotionally disconnected, Samuel's actions were seen as less affectionate; at times, he would stop opening doors for Andrea or may have left her alone where he would normally protect her. These actions were met with frustration by Andrea, beginning a non-verbal war until someone said enough was enough. Typically, Samuel would try to stop the war first because of his upbringing as described earlier, but the truth of the matter is that we both do not like to fight.

Here is an example that illustrates that we needed help. We were fighting about something that was not really important, but whatever the fight was about turned into the straw that broke the camel's back. In response to the argument, Andrea left the house to get some space to think and went shopping to make herself feel better. Samuel was attempting to reach her to talk about the argument, but the call was declined. She was not answering his phone calls because she was upset with him. In return, Samuel got frustrated with Andrea. He left the house and she stayed gone; these actions made the situation worse. Eventually, Andrea picked up the phone to talk. In that moment, we can't remember who said what, but one of us stated, "Remember that we vowed early in our marriage that we would never leave the house upset with each other. Instead, we could go anywhere in the house and the other person would respect the required space." We realized that we needed God's help!

Our Problems and God's Answers

Our problems started with expressed unresolved hurt and pain from within. God's answers helped to heal us from the inside out. God's Word and His spirit soothed our discomfort from the depths of our souls. Through the act of listening for His guidance by interacting with the Word and through prayer, we found the relief that was badly needed.

We turned again to Apostle Paul and listened to Apostle Peter, King Solomon, and our savior Jesus Christ this time, and used their examples to help us address our unresolved conflict. Their experiences and insights challenged us to stop fighting and start loving each other, because life is too short to play petty games with each other. Embracing the positivity instead of having a negative perspective allowed us to apply these kingdom insights into our marriage.

God's Word and His spirit soothed our discomfort from the depths of our souls.

Problems with identifying the non-verbal cues. Not identifying what was behind the non-verbal cues caused us to miss the sweet spot in our marriage for quite a while. With us putting our guard up, as we prepared for the next fight, we did not hear each other, but only heard our individual hurt and pain. God's answers in His Word are limitless and spoke to our hearts again but revealed something different in the same scripture we reviewed before. This time, we found ourselves being addressed by Apostle Paul again but illuminating our current situation. According to Romans 12:3-5, "every part supplies the whole," as Paul suggested that while we may serve different functions, such as a hand and a foot; however, we are both important. The essence of Paul's argument was that everyone was important to the body of Christ, translating that we are important to each other and our marriage. Paul's insight challenged us to take the positive mentality of the glass is half full that caused us to be more sensitive to each other's needs versus ignoring them.

Apostle Peter also challenged us to do better in our marriage. 1 Peter 4:8 conveyed constant effort was required in loving each other. This repeated message from 1 Peter 1:22 was important to Simeon Peter, particularly as this disciple of Christ encouraged the persecuted Christians in the Roman Empire to love one another. In this letter, Peter passed on hard-earned lessons from his imprisonment in the book of Acts. Although, his message was geared towards helping Christians trying to overcome suffering, this lesson motivated us to shift our perspective from enduring each other's faults to loving each other through our problems.

Problems with respecting each other's feelings when communicating. Respecting each other required putting aside our feelings of unresolved hurt and pain. Yes, putting your partner first or even considering their feelings is difficult when you feel like being in survivor mode and putting yourself first. Instead, changing our position required not only studying His Word, but also applying the scriptures to our situation. Proverbs 15:1 urged us to speak with our hearts and not out of anger as this passage states, "A soft answer turns away wrath, but grievous words stir up anger." King Solomon illustrated how to deal with conflict and avoiding an unhealthy environment. Solomon's statement made us focus on creating a safe environment rather than a toxic one. In this place of trust, we were able to see the intentions behind the non-verbal actions and hear our spouse's heart allowing us to communicate more effectively.

Proverbs 15:1 urged us to talk with our hearts and not our anger . . .

Another aspect of Solomon's wisdom assisted us with increasing effective communication encouraging us to gain respect for ourselves but, most importantly, respect for our marriage. Solomon, David's son, challenged his listeners to consider another way instead of a harsh answer. Such an act could foster a different response, as love. The love that Andrea has for Samuel helped her realize that when she ignored him, it caused more conflict in the marriage; this helped her begin to apply the true meaning of Proverbs 15:1. By Andrea giving a soft answer, even when she wanted to remain quiet, it helped Samuel remain calm and willing to talk. Learning to have balance helped us improve communication, but most of all, it has helped to improve our marriage.

Problems with building effective communication. Misidentifying non-verbal cues and disrespecting each other hindered our ability to communicate effectively. Our challenges resulted in different styles of managing conflict, resulting in a breakdown in communication and losing the intended message. Conventional wisdom states to be successful in marriage one needs to focus on their needs; however, King Solomon offered a different perspective from his experience with establishing the *Golden Age of Israel*, lasting 40 years. Proverbs 16:24 provided insight into perhaps how Solomon navigated the complexity of obtaining peace with his neighboring kingdoms as he expanded his influence; pleasant words can soothe the soul. His example of success urged us to examine how we talked to each other and managed conflict between us, challenging us to be more cautious and deliberate with our word choices.

Jesus's words also hit home in a big way. In John 15:13, Jesus described a new concept of friendship, from a biblical stand-point, of laying his life down for another. This concept was similar to Paul's statement in Ephesians 5:25, implying that a husband should be willing to die for his wife, as Christ did for all of us. Therefore, Jesus challenged us to not *compete* with each other but *complete* each other as friends. If we truly loved each other, we could look past each other's faults and grow our marriage into a lifelong friendship. Ultimately, we should become each other's best friend, building a deep and intimate relationship while accepting each other for ourselves.

Marriage Lessons

Communication is a very important part of a relationship. Putting an emphasis on the non-verbal communication, helped us truly understand how the other communicated. One of the most essential lessons that we learned from detailing our communication was how to connect with each other. By beginning to understand the non-verbal language the other spoke, we learned how to gauge when the other person's frustration level was at the breaking point.

Putting an emphasis on the non-verbal communication, helped us truly understand how the other communicated.

Recognizing our mistakes on how we communicated with each other made it easier for us to acknowledge that we look at each other as best friends. Thus, making it easier for us to talk in general. As a result, we were more willing to listen to each other's point-of-view and became more receptive to the other's suggestions. Our newfound level of communication also made it much easier for us to make difficult decisions without having significant conflict or opposition from the other.

Marriage lessons on identifying the non-verbal cues. Body language is an essential aspect of communication that is often misinterpreted or misunderstood. Knowing the way your spouse communicates non-verbally is a key to avoiding arguments and building stronger communication. Making your spouse's non-verbal communication a priority increases the effectiveness of verbal communication.

Marriage lessons on respecting each other's feelings when communicating. Learning to respect each other's feelings and thoughts is significant when working towards a healthy relationship. Sometimes it is difficult to understand what the other is feeling, especially if you are responding emotionally and you want your feelings and or thoughts to be heard. However, having open communication with your spouse, no matter how uncomfortable it may be, will improve how your spouse views you and considers your feelings.

Marriage lessons on building effective communication. The ability to communicate both verbally and non-verbally is important. Using non-verbal communication as a form of expression often contributes to confusion. Whereas being more vocal and having open communication with your spouse helps lead to healthier interactions. Managing conflict is not a contact sport; it is a labor of love that translates into the ultimate friendship that lasts a lifetime.

With these unique lessons under our belt, other couples' experiences may not coincide with ours, and that is ok. While it is true that everyone has their own experience, it may not necessarily address our common theme. In our lesson, it is truly knowing your spouse that ultimately leads to better communication. Any experiences not aimed at knowing and understanding how your spouse prefers to communicate may not only lead to friction, but also could end up forming a gulf between each person that is too big to bridge. Therefore, increasing effective communication could contribute to the advancement in your relationship.

Hence, communication is a vital part of any relationship. Having the insight needed to understand how your spouse communicates adds to the richness of your marriage. Identifying non-verbal cues, valuing each other's feelings, and acknowledging each other as friends are essential in providing the security needed for open lines of communication.

Having the insight needed to understand how your spouse communicates adds to the richness of your marriage.

Leadership Insights

Adam highlighted what not to do so that we could apply God's insights to our problems. God told Adam to stay away from the tree of knowledge of good and evil; if you eat of that tree you will die (Gen. 2:16-17). The guidelines were clear; however, these instructions did not get passed to Eve. God told him these instructions in Chapter 2 of Genesis and, according to the scriptures, Eve was not created until Chapter 3. Therefore, Adam had the responsibility to pass this critical information to his wife but failed to communicate the importance of what God said. As Adam struggled with communicating to Eve, we understand the importance and the consequences of poor communication. In Genesis 3:3, we see the difference in the instructions as Eve's response to the serpent:

- Concerning the fruit of the tree
  - In the garden
- God said
  - You shall not eat it
  - Nor shall you touch it
  - Lest you die

Learning from Adam's mistake, we noted a couple of things relating to communication. Although we did not know, for sure, if or how Adam missed Eve's non-verbal cues, we are sure of the result of miscommunication. Eve did not know the details of God's message, and Adam did not take responsibility for his poor communication. The serpent confused Eve, by telling her, you will not *surely* die (Gen. 3:4). The subtle difference in tone of what God said or did not say was enough to confuse Eve about the instructions that Adam received from God in Genesis Chapter 2. From Adam's example, God reinforced that we need to dial-in and to pay closer attention to each other because the details matter. Simply put, Adam underestimated the consequences. We see that his failure is something we can avoid through paying attention to non-verbal cues, resulting in better communication.

Leadership insights on identifying the non-verbal cues. Paying attention to the non-verbal details matter. Ensuring alignment with your spouse's thoughts helps to not only communicate better but to avoid confusion, as with Adam.

Identifying some of these non-verbal cues can be as simple as seeing facial expressions: happy, sad, anger, and fear or understanding your spouse's body language and posture indicating attitude, such as defensive postures of arm-crossing. There are some harder cues to detect as determining moods from your love one's appearance. As you spend more time together, these cues are easier to pick up.

Leadership insights on respecting each other's feelings when communicating. Get closer to know what your spouse is thinking or feeling is important. Such closeness may resolve uncertainty that may surface between both of you. Receiving clarity adds to the lack of confusion. As in the example with Adam and Eve, reducing ambiguity is what could have helped Eve.

The key to getting close is being present. Some practical ways of getting close are asking each other personal questions, showing interest in the things they like, working out together, or saying I love you more. Being present is more than physically sharing the same space; it is also being emotionally available.

Leadership insights on building effective communication. Building effective communication may be difficult if you don't pay attention to your spouse's reaction. Becoming an effective communicator requires not only what was mentioned above, but also making communication a priority, keeping your message simple and consistent, developing your listening skills, and maintaining eye contact to name a few. Combining these skills will increase your ability to become more of an effective communicator and avoid unnecessary pitfalls.

Some people may not believe that Adam's lessons or God's insights for us are on point or even necessary. We often say everyone is entitled to their opinion; however, a point that needs emphasized is there are consequences for one's actions. Therefore, maintaining open communication could help mitigate such challenges. Simply put, such consequences can be avoided through effective communication.

Therefore, every couple must underscore the importance of communication in their marriage. The difficult part is cutting through the noise and the clutter of life to hear your spouse clearly. Although this may be hard, clarity is needed for a relationship to be on one accord not only with each other, but also with God. Embracing God's alignment allows you and your spouse to reach a deeper place of communication which is from the soul, promoting the ability to move in the same direction.

Therefore, every couple must underscore the importance of communication in their marriage.

Conclusion

As noted at the beginning of this chapter, the lack of non-verbal communication between couples allows the opportunity to look at this challenge from different viewpoints. From our experiences, we have seen a theme of not truly understanding the intention of the non-verbal cues used, triggering a non-verbal war between us. As we remembered vital promises made in a calm time, these same promises guided us through the difficult times. Such guideposts paved the way for us to hear from God, so that we could clearly apply ourselves with God's answers to our problems.

As we went deep into our relationship, we saw God's lessons and insights. We experienced the negative side of fighting with each other; by paying closer attention to each other, we enjoyed a new level of happiness and trust. Leadership insights allowed us to see the importance of effective communication and understand how bad the consequences can be if we ignore God's message. The open lines of communication established in this chapter paves the way in Chapter 4 to help with resolving conflict in healthy ways. Below are some questions designed to help with opening the lines of communication wider in your marriage.

QUESTIONS FOR REFLECTION
AND DISCUSSION

1. **Identifying the Non-Verbal Cues**—How do you communicate with your spouse non-verbally? What are some of the challenges that you have faced in your relationship because of non-verbal communication? How would you say the challenges that you had with your spouse with non-verbal communication improved your ability to communicate?

2. **Respecting Each Other's Feelings When Communicating**—How do you deal with managing conflict? In what ways would you say you have disregarded spouse's feelings when communicating? What have you learned as a result of your spouse's response when he / she felt undervalued regarding his / her feelings?

3. **Building Effective Communication**—How would you define effective communication in your marriage? What are some steps that you can take to ensure that you effectively communicate with your spouse? What is one thing that you are willing to commit to help increase effective communication within your marriage?

CHAPTER 4.

CONFLICT IS GOOD: HEALTHY WAYS TO DEAL WITH CONFLICT

Throughout our marriage we fought; sometimes it was bad. After reflecting, we realized that our understanding of how to use the tools of resolution were inadequate when handling the problems we faced. The literature indicates that we are not alone, and the results are disheartening. As referenced by the Center for Disease Control and Prevention (CDC, 2019), approximately 1 of 5 women and 1 of 7 men are identified as victims of physical violence from a significant other. These statistics highlight not only that a big problem exists, but also prompts us to wonder if there is another way to deescalate problems within a marriage. Such prescriptive ways may not exist, however what we offer are alternative methods from our experiences, grounded in God's principles.

One of the marriage saving principles we used was never to go to bed angry with one another. Apostle Paul wrote from prison to the Ephesians, conveying his view on anger. He penned in Ephesians 4:26, "Be ye angry, and sin not: let not the sun go down upon your wrath," which helped us. Some often think that conflict is not good, but we beg to differ. When we became upset with each other, we tried to implement Paul's principles as often as we could; however, there were some instances where we fell short. In each situation, we tried to learn from the conflict and make improvements.

One of the marriage saving principles we used was never to go to bed angry with one another.

Conflict is good because of the ability to help a person learn how to deal with another better, especially in a committed relationship. You learn what makes the person angry, frustrated, sad, etc. and vice versa. However, just as Paul spoke to the early Christians, he spoke to us; it is not good to remain upset for too long. No one wants anything bad to happen to a loved one and you are unable to ask for forgiveness. In the midst of conflict, we found a way of escape through God.

As we navigate through this chapter, we address the healthy and unhealthy ways we have dealt with conflict. In addition, we illuminate the experiences we had in balancing ministry and family. While exposing the way we managed healthy and unhealthy ways to confront conflict, we also explore the significance of acknowledging your significant other's love language.

Learn from the Bad Ways to Deal with Conflict

After being married for 20 plus years, we have a number of unhealthy responses to our arguments and disagreements. Contained in our responses were not only hurtful actions, but also some disappointments from how we reacted to bad situations, causing things to become worse in some cases. We experienced the effect that difficult decisions had on our family when it came to trying to protect us from the feelings of hurt and pain or shutting down. Even as a family, we shut everyone out to heal in a safe environment. We went inward as detailed below.

We shut down and cut off some friends, family, coworkers, and church members because life overwhelmed us. As God is the center of our lives, we confused loving Him with serving man. Being a leader at church is a great joy, as well as serving God's people. The problem was that we overextended ourselves with working with multiple ministries within a church. We were confused because we thought we were doing great things for the Lord, but we became out of balance with our obligations, our relationships, and our home suffered.

Recognizing that overcommitment was a problem, we examined other areas of our lives for similar work-life conflicts. To our surprise, these imbalanced areas existed from multiple family gatherings and friends' obligations to fraternity and sorority functions and work activities; not to mention three additional schedules from our active children, their school, sports and social calendar events. Life was hectic and we wanted to scream; our kids needed us, and we needed each other!

We did the next best thing and shut the overcommitment and confusion down! We stopped all the extra activities we could and focused on family. Understanding when to say no, often presented a challenge, especially when working with the things we love. We understand that ministry begins in the home, and if the home is not in order, it will be difficult to serve in the church or anywhere else. A period of rest and recalibration was needed.

We had to come to an agreement on how to navigate our convictions as individuals and as a family. At various points throughout our interaction with the ministry, there have been instances where Samuel overextended himself and Andrea had to intervene. She challenged him on the fact the family needed more of him, especially as the kids continued to get older. There were also times where Andrea overextended, and Samuel had to interject and provide balance. Interestingly, his plea was on the same grounds as Andrea's, the family needs you. Therefore, overextending ourselves in, various instances, contributed to many disagreements where we responded poorly.

Sadly, as we turned inward for protection, we began to fight against each other. The arguments we found ourselves engaging in often led to not speaking throughout the day and even going to church upset with each other while not hiding our frustration well at all. This was extremely unhealthy because we were letting others in on our personal matters, but most of all, our children could see the disconnect between the two of us. Furthermore, our irritation with one another made it easier for others to comment on what they saw. Outsiders intervening in our relationship made it easier to distance ourselves by taking on more tasks or avoiding communicating with each other, which was not good. Simply put, we struggled to communicate to others that we needed space for a season and to say no; this caused frustration in our house and we took our anger out on each other.

The arguments we found ourselves engaging in often led to not speaking throughout the day . . .

Our experience illustrated what not to do. With a conflict between serving man in the House of the Lord and our family, we chose God and family. We wanted to please God and make Him proud of us. We had to answer the question, how? We realized we had to establish a more effective way to operate by ensuring our household and our children were taken care of and they received the attention they needed. Also needed to ensure we gave each other the attention the other needed and other family obligations were met as we moved forth with supporting leadership within the ministry. Eventually we began to understand that we were not giving all that we should give to God because in some cases, we were giving to several ministries and organizations while feuding with each other. We began to realize that we needed to maintain a healthy balance and find another way to deal with our conflict.

Focus on the Good Ways to Deal with Conflict

We realized that we needed to listen to one another instead of disagreeing so much. We recognized that we were not each other's enemy and there was a way that we could accomplish both, serving God and balancing our family. The focus on maintaining structure within our household made it easier for us to fulfill obligations in ministry while focusing on identifying things we could do to help us to remain on one accord.

The importance of spending quality time together outside of other obligations was highlighted throughout this process. We realized the importance of scheduling time for each other as a couple and time with our family. Once the schedule was created, we committed to adhering to it. On most occasions, the only thing that we would adjust our schedule for was an emergency.

*We realized the importance of scheduling time for
each other as a couple and time with our family.*

We began to see the difference. As we maintained more balance, there were fewer arguments and less confusion between us. Balance also improved our ability to effectively communicate with each other and avoid allowing our frustration to show if we did have a disagreement. Now, we were self-aware and tried to improve our actions in public.

Recognizing the impact high levels of frustration had on how others perceived our relationship or what we may have been going through also prepared us for further interaction in ministry. Our undying love for God compelled us to start our own ministry. We acknowledged that as future leaders, we have to be an example to others. Learning from our previous experiences and identifying healthier ways to manage conflict in ministry, continues to play a part in our development as leaders.

Understanding Your Spouse's Love Language

Everybody has a love language. Gary Chapman (2015) described five love languages as (a) word of affirmation, using words to affirm others; (b) acts of service, actions speak louder than words; (c) receiving gifts, feeling love from gifts; (d) quality time, giving others your attention; and (e) physical touch, receiving appropriate touching. From these five, we used some and added our own. Ultimately, we learned how to speak to our spouse in a way that makes them feel appreciated, specifically in two ways.

The first is giving to each other in ways unique to us. We love each other and love doing things for each other. When we thought about our expressions of love, we each have our way of doing things for the other person that brings us joy. Interestingly, both of us like to show love by doing acts of service. Samuel likes to make sure Andrea is looked after. For example, filling up her car with gas because she hates pumping gas or simply taking all the change and paper out of his pockets before she does the laundry, which frees her up from checking pockets before washing clothes.

Andrea for instance, likes to make sure Samuel feels secure in how much she loves him, and she shows it by performing acts of kindness. She may run his bath water, rub him down with alcohol after a rough day of work, or cooking his favorite meal. The common thread between us is that we show love by taking care of each other through our actions. Our ability to show love is really in the simple things, now. The beginning of marriage was different because we had to learn to trust each other with our whole hearts. Trust between us makes loving each other simple and adds to the affection we show towards each other.

The second way is based on how we like to receive affection. Samuel loves to receive words of affirmation from his wife. Receiving these words helps him to feel valued and loved. Some examples of Andrea's words of thanks and appreciations are for taking her car to get fixed, taking her to lunch after she left her lunch at home, or taking the kids to medical appointments because she is the one who usually takes them. These encouraging words and actions helped to strengthen the bond between us beyond touch. As Andrea demonstrates her love for Samuel, he also shows that he too can return the favor.

For Andrea, being listened to and not just heard is what Samuel can do to make her feel loved. Not only does sharing her heart with him matter, but also allowing her voice to be heard and strengthen a place of no judgment. Because Andrea has difficulties expressing herself verbally, at times, Samuel honoring her love language is more important than receiving gifts. However, Samuel is doing his best to make sure that his wife does not miss her share of gifts. This is truly love in action because Samuel likes to save money more than spending it.

Whether giving or receiving love, it is important to find your unique path to love and grow together. Although being listened to is not one of the five love languages described by Chapman (2015), it is a love language for Andrea that Samuel enjoys making come true. The point is that our love is tailor-made between us, which makes it special. Each couple cannot be afraid to find their own path towards love. Sometimes that road is hidden, requiring hard work to create a path where it does not exist.

Our Problems and God's Answers

Our challenges stemmed from our inability to stay properly balanced, our inability to manage our obligations, and our inability to consider each other's feelings. In the midst of our confusion, God provided guidance through His Word and examples through scripture. With divine messengers such as Apostle Paul, King Solomon, and Apostle Peter, the Holy Spirit illuminated their time locked insights into sage wisdom that helped us correct the unhealthy ways of dealing with conflict and maintain the healthy ways with better communication. These biblical leaders' experiences and insights challenged us to love not only each other, but also our family, because our kids deserve more from us. Finding our path truly led us to find the happiness that God designed for us in our own way.

*Our challenges stemmed from our inability
to stay properly balanced . . .*

Problems with unhealthy ways to deal with conflict. Responding to conflict in unhealthy ways, highlighted some internal and external problems. We faced concerns with our inability to manage our time with additional obligations outside of our family unit. Considering our unwavering desire to please God, we had to come to a compromise. When Apostle Paul wrote to the city of Corinth in his 1st letter, he detailed that God is not the author of confusion, but of peace (1 Cor. 14:33). Paul argued that things should be done decently and in order, which adds value to the church. As he rebuked the church for being in disorder, Paul also challenged us to get our own house in order. His strong words hit home, causing us to seek God. Our love for God pushed us to put our house in order, so that His will be done for our family.

Paul urged us to stop the madness from prison in his letter to the Christians at Ephesus. Ephesians 4:31-32 conveyed to get rid of the bitterness, anger, and shouting insults, instead the message was to be kind and loving just as Christ has forgiven you. This message was for us and it seemed like Paul was in our house, his message convinced us not to do wrong towards each other. Paul challenged the Ephesians and us in the same way, as he was trying to build teamwork amidst adversity. This lesson motivated us to find another way to get rid of selfishness and to come together as one.

Problems with healthy conflict resolution. Learning to specify healthy solutions when facing conflict was difficult because we did not establish the importance of acknowledging the other's point-of-view when we faced conflict. We know that according to Philippians 4:7, "And the peace of God, which passeth all understanding, shall keep your hearts and minds through Christ Jesus." Apostle Paul wrote from a Roman prison, never losing his sense of purpose to God's mission. With this frame of mind, Paul urged his readers to maintain focus on the right things and discipline to the things of God. His call to focus helped us to do the same in our marriage with love and grace, seeking out healthy ways to deal with conflict and providing a roadmap that we were able to work towards, establishing boundaries to gain a higher level of understanding balance.

In addition, King Solomon provided us with another great point in the book of wisdom. Proverbs 15:18 cautioned us about hot tempers that cause arguments; instead we should show patience which brings peace. Solomon distilled wisdom that shifts one's mindset, specifically in leaders. He urged his readers not to respond in anger or in a violent manner, because their calm or patient ways can absorb a person's fury. His words evoked us not to fight rather to find healthy ways to deal with anger in ourselves and others. Solomon's call to action helped influence us to resolve conflict in a healthy way.

Problems with understanding love languages. The challenges of being married are incomparable and difficult, to say the least. Mature couples who truly understand one another have achieved an important milestone. Our inability to connect with each other using the other's love language was simply because they were unknown to us. Proverbs 4:7 conveyed, that wisdom should be received first and with all thy getting get understanding. King Solomon built on his father, King

David's, teaching of gaining wisdom and understanding (Prov. 4:3); therefore, nothing in life was more important, than knowing God's wisdom and responding correctly to life's challenges. As Solomon built on his father's insight, we were urged to develop our marriage, becoming stronger in our bond and more knowledgeable of each other so we can respond as a team, to life's challenges.

The challenges of being married are incomparable and difficult.

Next, Apostle Peter reminded us about God's sweet spot of marriage. 1 Peter 3:1-7 described leadership in the home by the wife submitting to her husband and the husband understanding his wife, modeling honor through submission and service. Peter helped us to realize that to truly honor each other, we needed to communicate in a way that allowed us to understand the other's heart. Hearing our heart's concerns through our love language pushed us closer and more in synchronization with each other. The closer we became, the easier it was to honor our marriage and move beyond our problems.

Marriage Lessons

Conflict is good. This may be confusing to some. However, something to consider is, if you do not have conflict, how will you know what makes your spouse upset? Understanding what your spouse's breaking point is will help you manage your response to your spouse in future disagreements.

The extent of our disagreements was very extreme in the beginning of our marriage. However, as we have grown together, we learned how to avoid conflict. For instance, we came to an understanding that it would be best to give each other space to calm down and avoid communicating something that we may regret. Learning healthy ways to manage conflict helped us grow closer in our marriage.

> *However, as we have grown together, we learned how to avoid conflict.*

Marriage lessons on unhealthy ways to deal with conflict. Not prioritizing our responsibilities properly caused confusion and chaos. Serving God is not the same as serving man. Therefore, evoking insights from 1 Timothy 5:8, leadership begins at home, then goes outward. Refocusing our relationship priorities as God, spouse, kids, and ministry aligned us with God's plan.

Marriage lessons on healthy conflict resolution. Talking *to* each other and not talking *at* each other was essential in our ability to deal with conflict. We began to listen to each other, and that increased our level of communication. Better communication allowed us to work through conflict more quickly and more effectively.

Marriage lessons on understanding love languages. The key to unlocking the deepest connection with your spouse is understanding their love language. Using each other's love language caused us to grow stronger as a married couple. Learning how to communicate with each other in time of conflict, enhanced our ability to resolve conflict quickly.

Some couples may not agree with our hard-earned marriage

lessons. Although their path maybe different than ours, we feel that our lessons embodied fundamental items which should not be ignored. On the one hand, we agree that couples with their experiences may prefer focusing on their careers, ministry, or other obligations, which enables them to enjoy well deserved success. But on the other hand, we still insist that you can have both (success and family), just not at the expense of sacrificing one over the other. This approach takes being on accord with the family's priorities in mind.

In short, healthy responses to conflict enhance the love in a marriage compared to unhealthy actions against a spouse. Having the insight of your spouse's love language makes communication interesting, personal, and fun, enriching the bonds of trust and friendship that builds deep intimacy. Finding your spouse's love language is not only critical, but also important to a long-lasting marriage.

Leadership Insights

We gained insight from our marriage experiences, learning from God's leadership through Apostle Paul, as he pushed through adversity in the city of Corinth. In a second letter to the Corinthians, Paul penned a defense of his character, a challenge to overcome being a fractured community of believers, and how to straighten a broken moral compass. As this church's founder, Paul spoke from a father's heart; he was disappointed. He plead, rebuked, and wept with the Corinthian Christian community for their future. Just as Paul, we had to find a healthy way to confront our challenges so we could have a brighter future.

---

*We gained insight from our marriage experiences,
learning from God's leadership . . .*

We saw ourselves in Paul's struggle. As he defended his church, we defended our family. 2 Corinthians 11:16-28 stated that Paul defended his ministry and his leadership by answering his critics. With Paul's record for Christ, he would be a fool to enter into a debate with other leaders against him, but he did. His audience was the community he founded, diverse with men, women, slaves, free, Jew, and Gentiles, which was a sample of the influence in the port city. His 2nd letter set the record straight by outlining his track record of suffering for Christ (2 Cor. 11:22-28):

- I am a Hebrew; I am Israelite; I am a minister of Christ

- I have worked harder, look at my stripes from the Jews,
  - 5 times, I have received 39 stripes
  - 3 times, I was beaten by rods
  - Once, I was stoned

- 3 times, I was shipwrecked, a night and day deep at sea

- Across my journeys,
  - I faced danger from waters, robbers, my people, in the cities,
  - the Gentiles, in the wilderness, false brothers, sleeplessness,
  - cold and naked, hunger and thirst, and fasting

- I am not weak!

Paul's defense strengthens us! If he could defend himself, then we could defend our marriage. The fact that Paul won the argument showed us that we can let our record speak for itself. As we look back, we have a long track record with God that not only encourages us, but also illustrates our faithfulness. We love God and refocused on taking care of our family and each other. His leadership inspired us to look at our family in a different way. Paul as a father stood up for his church and reminded them of his track recorded. First, we reminded ourselves of our track record with God. Then, we focused on family then outward to satisfy other obligations. Acknowledging Paul's insight allowed us to apply these lessons to or marriage.

Leadership insights on unhealthy ways to deal with conflict. Remembering our track record with God helps us to see what is important. Prioritizing the important things to God and our family, reduces friction points between us because of alignment.

Prioritizing what is important can be difficult; this depends on the couple's mindset. Being on one accord is key to establishing a focus, required for designing a doable list for the family. When creating such a list, make sure to collect all the tasks; separate urgent from important, rank the most important on the top to the less important on the bottom, and agree on the list.

Leadership insights on healthy conflict resolution. Properly aligning God's plan with your family's track record is an opportunity to talk with each other and work together. Being goal focused, not only helps with communications, it also helps with vision planning for the family. Working as a family towards a goal also reduces conflict in the house.

Talking with each other is the key to working together. Looking each other in the eyes, listening actively, using their names, making them feel important, and emphasizing similarities with your loved one are ways of communicating. These examples imply that a couple must be mentally present for things to work. The synergy created from being present may lead to new insights that could create a deep bond between the couple.

Leadership insights on understanding love languages. Working together produces unity and harmony that paves the way for a deeper connection. Enhancing this bond through meaningful communication of love languages has the benefits of a stronger marriage that can weather storms, reach higher heights, and accomplish more goals together.

Working together produces unity and harmony that paves the way for a deeper connection.

Finding out each other's love languages can be fun. Spending time and asking interesting questions can assist in discovering what may be an unknown love language. Questions like, how do you like to receive love outside of sex or what makes you happy by doing X for me? Understanding these answers can bring you closer in ways that you never thought of before.

These powerful insights helped us; some couples might not see the value. Others may experience an alternate path in different direction. For instance, a solo approach rather than the team approach could be detrimental to a marriage. Aligning the lone ranger mindset with the family's goals may be difficult. Such an isolation method may be difficult to align to a family and one person's goals. Being in a single mindset hinders the growth within the family unit. According to Ephesians 4:16, "Every part supplies the whole." All parts are needed to work together in order for success to be a factor.

In summary, it is important that understanding healthy conflict resolution is critical to a strong marriage. Having the insight to use the track record with God helps put the future into perspective. Working together secures the future, with love and closeness. This is a journey of love focused on goals, which keeps the marriage strong.

Conclusion

This chapter addressed the issue of how to deal with conflict, resulting in a reduction of work-life conflict and a tailor-made love language. From our experiences, we realized that ensuring the home is taken care of aids with expanding influence among one's jobs, ministries, and passions. We also saw that developing an authentic love language aids with taking care of the important relationships at home. With our experiences firmly in hand, we turned towards God to assist us with applying His solutions to our problems through advice found in scripture.

We were excited to see how God's lessons and insights took us to another level in our marriage. God showed us how to respond to our spouse through love and respect, leading to a deeper intimacy between us. He reminded us about remembering God's proven track record, in our marriage, as a way to look towards the future and to ignore the negative voices; such a resolve is needed, as reflected in Chapter 5, to make intimacy work. Below are some thought provoking questions to help think about your relationship as related to dealing with conflict.

*God showed us how to respond to our
spouse through love and respect . . .*

QUESTIONS FOR REFLECTION
AND DISCUSSION

1. **Unhealthy ways to deal with conflict**—When you reflect on your marriage, what are some unhealthy ways that you and your spouse deal with conflict? What are some things that you noticed in yourself when the conflict was not managed in a healthy way? What are some things that you noticed in your spouse when the conflict was not resolved in a constructive manner?

2. **Healthy conflict resolution**—How have you been able to improve your marriage by handling conflict in a healthy way? What are some things that you may have done differently to improve the conflict resolution even more? If you could help your spouse understand how he / she has helped with your ability to resolve conflict in your marriage, what would you say to him / her?

3. **Understanding love languages**—What is your love language? How can you apply the knowledge of your love language to improving your relationship with your spouse? What would you say your spouse's love language is and why?

Chapter 5.

MAKING LOVE COUNT: INTIMACY

Our intimacy was on a never-ending roller-coaster ride. When it was great, it was awesome; when it was not, it sucked! One of the biggest challenges couples face is intimacy and how do they maintain it! In 2019, research indicated that 92% of people are more sexually attracted to their partner if their partner shows vulnerability (Stritof, 2020). Too often sex is confused with intimacy and many couples miss the mark because one or both of individuals are not emotionally connected, which causes a breakdown in intimacy. Sex is based on physical gratification and intimacy is based on something much deeper, being emotionally connected with someone close. Realizing that sex and intimacy are not the same may help some couples understand how to build upon true intimacy. In this chapter, we explore sex compared to intimacy in more detail.

Too often sex is confused with intimacy and many couples miss the mark because one or both of individuals are not emotionally connected . . .

Acknowledging the challenges we faced with intimacy helped us to improve drastically. Some of the measures we took were to honor and value each other. We made it a point to enjoy each other with outings at home and going out-of-town. We began to find ways to improve our love life during our private time; this played a significant role in increasing our physical and spiritual connection.

Being equally yoked within a marriage is a significant aspect of building intimacy. One specific aspect that helped create a more intense level of intimacy was the goal that we began together and accomplished together. Early in our relationship, it was determined that a PhD was the ultimate goal in relation to educational achievements. Chapter 5 covers our problems with honoring each other as king and queen, making time for each other, as well as making love and spicing up the love life, illustrating that couples can enjoy the best of one another.

Honoring Each Other as King and Queen

The realization that as a married couple the wife is the queen and the husband is the king adds to the level of compassion and intimacy. We recognized that within a marriage, it was important to keep in mind that we vowed to be partners for life. Acknowledging each other through compliments, respecting each other' feelings, and embracing the strengths of your spouse helps to solidify your bond and your roles within your marriage.

Once the connection that should be established in marriage has been acknowledged, giving each other compliments becomes easier. Letting the other know that you notice qualities about them that enhance them as a person increases the bond that you have with one another. One of Samuel's qualities is that he compliments Andrea and always tells her that he loves her and how proud he is to have her as his wife. When he does offer compliments, the gesture goes a long way. The nice words make it easier for Andrea to show her love for him both through public action and in the bedroom. Through the genuine compliments, the connection strengthens, and respect was established even the more.

Respect is a fundamental aspect of the relationship. It is so easy for married couples to become comfortable with each other and lose respect for one another. We often feel that the ones we love and whom we know love us will always be there. Well, we hate to burst your bubble, but that is nowhere near the case. One of the things Andrea had to learn was the importance of respecting Samuel as her husband and the head of their household. She had to learn to honor him as her husband. In addition, Samuel learned to respect Andrea as his wife and embrace her differences. As we began to mature, we leaned on Ephesians 4:16 emphasizing every part supplies the whole, that is when we began to notice things start to shift in a good way even more.

There is no big U in marriage, literally. However, we all have strengths that can complement our spouse. Once again referencing both of us earning our PhDs, there was never a competition. Andrea's strength in focusing on achieving the highest academic degree that she could helped motivate Samuel to move forward and encouraged him to achieve the same. Andrea's strength, in this example, helped to compensate for one of the struggles that Samuel faced with education and helped motivate him to strive and continue his education. Through this example, we continue to illuminate the fact that in marriage, there should not be a fight against the other person's will or trying to hinder your spouse's progress because you don't have the same aspirations. That is simply not fair!

There is no big U in marriage, literally.

Ascending to the throne. We viewed the blissful state of our marriage as king and queen. This journey was long and hard; it reminded us of our PhD journey that was filled with many challenges. The ascension in our hearts and our home was viewed as a kingdom and the pathway to our credentials of Doctor of Philosophy were similar; both were like climbing a mountain. Our experiences of the good and the bad were worth exploring to understand how our resolve became strengthened between us as described below.

As we went higher, we got nervous. Neither of us have climbed a mountain of this magnitude before, but we knew that we had to face our goals and our fears. Facing the foothills challenged us differently; however, the path was still a long way towards accomplishing our educational goals. We started at the same point in college. Andrea began at Winston Salem State University (WSSU) and then transferred to Fayetteville State University (FSU), only taking her four and a half years to graduate. Whereas, Samuel took 8 years, starting out at FSU, where they met, transferring to multiple colleges until he finished at University of Phoenix, while stationed in Arizona.

Even though Andrea's journey took less time, she and Samuel had challenges. Andrea's challenges were being young trying to enjoy the life of a college student, and spending time with friends. There was a lack of focus on academics. However, when

Andrea became pregnant with our first child, out of wedlock, during her senior year, things changed. Our child motivated us in different ways. Andrea became focused and earned higher grades her last year and a half of school, while working in the evenings and nights. Samuel left school to join the U.S. Army for the benefits to take care of our family. Samuel's challenges also included finding schools that would take his credits. He had to attend school at night, working around being a soldier—training and deploying—making it more difficult to finish. Every step of the way, uncertainty existed of how our educational journey was going to turn out.

As we continued to climb, the air got a little thinner, causing us to become anxious. With our Bachelors' degrees in hand, we had to catch our breath. We had to get used to the air. For Samuel, the focus was on breaking barriers as the first one to graduate college in his family. Whereas, Andrea was meeting the standard set by her mother who is a retired nurse. Once, we realized we could operate at this level, Andrea's dream of earning a PhD urged them to keep going. Eventually, Samuel would obtain two Masters' degrees, and Andrea earned a teaching certification before earning her Master's degree.

The challenges of completing school did not stop us from furthering our education. From military trainings to combat zones to military institutions, Samuel endured the necessary hardships to earn his Master level degrees. As for Andrea, she was going to school at night, running a household often by herself, raising three kids, and climbing her career ladder while Samuel was away. She did not have it easy at all. Either way, our paths were filled with potholes and detours, causing us both to get frustrated and wanting to give up through the process, but we did not. Instead, we encouraged each other along the way.

We were not done! We had higher to climb in search of the mystical PhD. This journey took time, over 8 years from the start to cresting the peak of this mountain. As we went up, the air got so thin that we almost passed out. At times, Samuel and Andrea had to encourage each other not to give up because the climb was very steep. The rope we had sometimes could only support one of us; not two. One would have to take a couple steps ahead of the other and turn around to help the other one behind climb up the cliff. Through all the pain, scratches, and bruises, we soon forgot how difficult the journey was as we reached the top together. Looking below, we could see miles and miles around. We enjoyed the view. We screamed and jumped for joy, praising God for the grace. However, few heard us, and fewer saw us because not many ventured up that mountain. Our climb highlighted for us, our journey together, a goal that was set in Andrea's mind over 20 years ago, was finally reached, not only by her but Samuel as well.

We wanted each other to win, realizing when one of us won, we both won.

Reflecting on our climb and reaching our throne, we paused and thanked God. This climb illustrated milestones in our marriage. We observed four important milestones. At the 5-year mark, we survived having kids and fighting against each other. We did not like each other, and it showed. However, we did not give up on God. At the 10-year point, we started to respect each other and each other's boundaries, after many arguments and disagreements. We wanted each other to win, realizing when one of us won, we both won. At the 15-year mark, we empathized with each other's fears because we knew and lived through them. We truly did not want to see the other hurting, as our hearts turned towards each other. At the 20-year point, we were proud and willing to defend each other no matter if we were right or wrong. However, if one of us was wrong in his / her statement or action, the matter would be discussed privately and needed insight was provided to address the issue; when one of us was ready to deal with the issue, we knew we had the support of our spouse. At this moment, we crested the peak. Through this process, we truly saw each other as king and queen standing on top of the mountain. As we are admiring the view, interestingly enough, Samuel sees another mountain to climb and has his eyes on a degree for God, Andrea begins to also ponder another one. Whatever happens, we want to be together.

Making Quality Time Last at Home and Away

Your spouse is a part of you. The two of you are one. When you took vows before your family and God, you became one flesh. Treating your spouse as you would treat yourself is important. For ladies, some like to get away and be pampered, to include, getting their hair and nails done, going shopping, or whatever it is that helps find a sense of peace or relaxation. Men, may like to go into their man cave and watch sports, go golfing, hang out with friends, or whatever is chosen to do to create downtime for yourself. While your spouse needs that too, he / she also needs time with you. It is important that you find time to date during "everyday" activities, make time for weekend get-a-ways, and take a trip for your anniversary each year. Quality time with your spouse is valuable time that will create memories and help intensify intimacy.

Treating your spouse as you would treat yourself is important.

A regular trip to the grocery store could turn into one of the most romantic experiences that a couple could have. Many people would say that makes no sense. Consider this, quality time is quality time. Anything is what you make it. Husbands, when you pull into the parking spot at the grocery store, the simple gesture of opening the door for you wife is romantic. Wives, when entering the store, asking your husband to lead you to the sections where the foods are so that you can get the ingredients to prepare his favorite meal. As a couple, when you get in the store, the simple gesture of pushing the cart together and having meaningful conversation is a way to add to the experience. It does not take much to build intimacy, and there is always an opportunity to make a date out of any activity. Taking advantage of everyday activities as romantic events can help with the anticipation of more intentional get-a-ways such as taking a short weekend trip.

Two to three days can make a world of difference in the quality of your marriage. Getting away from the hustle and bustle of everyday life, raising children, working, and adhering to other obligations can be a stress reliever. To experience short times away with the one you love can serve as a way to help rejuvenate your relationship. Stepping away from "everyday" life spontaneously, often helps remind us that we need to reconnect with each other as we often get too comfortable with one another. Sometimes becoming too comfortable can make it easier to take advantage of your spouse and the love they have for you. As a married couple, it is very important to keep your relationship "fresh," and to celebrate your spouse!

Any reason to celebrate one another is important when creating intimacy and connection in your marriage. One very significant celebration is the ability to honor another year of being married to the same person and realize that you have the ability to continue to grow more and more in-love with that person. Anniversaries are very special, and it is essential to take time out to acknowledge that. Taking a trip away from home on your anniversary not only helps to commemorate the vows that you took as a couple, but it helps to reaffirm that you had faith enough in each other to keep going and not to give up. Not only will this increase physical intimacy, but it will help enhance emotional intimacy.

Making Love—Spicing up Your Love Life

Intimacy spans beyond the physical love making. One of the most common misnomers is that physically making love solves all problems, arguments, or disagreements. In some instances, making love temporarily pacifies the situation, but it does not resolve it. It is very clear that communication is essential to clarifying misunderstandings, but it is also important to understand other things that increase intimacy that are often unspoken. Husbands, it is important that you are selfless when it comes to creating intimacy with your wife. Wives, understanding the significance of making your husband feel respected and valued as a man is important when it comes to building intimacy with him.

One of the things that Andrea values from Samuel as his wife, is being a man who will provide security and protect her at all cost. In most cases, that requires him to be selfless. Through-out our marriage, it took time for us to get to the point where he was ready to fill that role. Not knowing if Samuel would protect her at any cost made her feel insecure and uncertain about their relationship; in turn, there was only a physical connection when they had private time and not intimacy. As the marriage progressed, and Samuel felt more obligated to fulfill the role of the protector, Andrea became more vulnerable, and the intimacy increased substantially. More meaningful intimacy was given and received.

Samuel has always been aware that it is his job to protect and provide security for his wife. However, there was something that he needed from his wife in order to feel connected to her intimately. He wanted to be respected and valued as the protector and provider. Early on in the marriage, there was a lack of respect on Andrea's part for Samuel. She did not value him as the provider and failed to accept it when he offered to protect her. This impacted the level of intimacy substantially. Samuel refused to give all of himself to Andrea. He was there physically, but he was absent emotionally. As time progressed, Andrea learned to acknowledge Samuel as the head of the household and respect him as a man; as he began to let down his guard, the intimacy from him increased dramatically.

Intimacy is not always about sex or physical contact; it is about being connected mentally and emotionally. As a married couple, when your spouse feels that he or she is being valued according to what is important to him / her, the level of connection from all aspects tends to improve. The reinforcement of security for women and the sense of feeling valued as a provider for most men are some of the things that we found helped increase the passion and intimacy within our marriage.

Our problems began within us, but we had a resource in God that provided us with the guidance we needed.

Our Problems and God's Answers

Our problems began within us, but we had a resource in God that provided us with the guidance we needed. We experienced challenges early in our marriage because we were so young, and we were trying to figure things out. We did not realize the importance of valuing each other as husband and wife. We were practically roommates who had to grow in love with one another. Among all of our confusion and discord, there was a source we were able to connect with to give us the guidance we needed to grow together as a married couple. We relied on our faith and direction from the Word of God.

We did not realize the importance of valuing each other as husband and wife.

Problems with not honoring each other as king and queen. It took time for us to get to the point where we were able to complement each other as a couple and appreciate the other as king and queen. We did not have the right connection because we were too busy trying to focus on our individual needs and not the needs of each other. Apostle Paul addressed this type of relationship from a different angle in Rome. Romans 12:10-20 conveyed the complexity of leadership relationships. Paul's message addressed being loyal, hospitable, and respectful, which helped us. Studying the gospel of Paul challenged our relationship to become strong as royalty. We are royalty and treating each other as such is a mindset that we must have.

Additionally, Paul encouraged us to do more because of others. Titus 2:1-7 described the art of mentorship. Paul wrote to his spiritual son Titus, trusting him with the tough assignments of fixing problems with churches. Paul's mentorship with Titus urged us to look at our children. As leaders of our house, we had an obligation to model and train our children to become better than us. Therefore, not honoring each other as a king and a queen or treating our kids as princes and a princess, violated the model. One day we will give our children a tough assignment to carry on our family legacy.

Problems with not making time for each other. Early in our marriage, we did not understand the value of spending time with each other and the difference that it made. There was a time in our marriage where we did not appreciate spending time with one another. We would rather have our own space. Apostle Paul helped us with his 2nd letter to the Thessalonians. 2 Thessalonians 3:5 implied, the Lord directs your hearts into God's love and Christ's perseverance. Paul's message was about getting back to the basics. We recognized that he was reminding us of dating and how much we used to spend time together, which was not the case then. This lack of observing the basics such as time, highlighted a vulnerability in our marriage that was an easy fix; spend time together!

Paul once again spoke to our situation. 2 Thessalonians 2:16-17 described hearts being encouraged and hearts being strengthened. From a lack of time spent together, these ingredients were missing from our marriage. As Paul led this young church of believers to correct their wrong thinking about Christ's return and overcoming their challenges with persecution, he urged us to adjust our mindsets and change our actions towards each other. The shift in mindset made it easier to spend time together because we too wanted our hearts to be encouraged and strengthened.

Problems with making love and spicing up the love life. We had difficulties honoring each other and fulfilling each other's needs, which impacted our ability to achieve high levels of intimacy. As we reflected on our shortcomings, it was obvious that we had some work to do when it came to our emotional connection. The unknown writer of Hebrew is sometimes debated as Apostle Paul, spoke to us. Hebrews 13:4 stated that marriage is honorable in all and the bed is undefiled. The writer addressed doctrinal issues challenging old Jewish mindsets to a better life. The unnamed author provided moral guidance in a day where sex was commonly practiced outside of marriage in an attempt to confine it to marriage. We expanded this message to increase our level of intimacy by being more emotional available to each other.

Apostle Paul showed us how to submit. Ephesians 5:21 described the importance of submitting to one another out of reverence for Christ. Paul challenged the Christians in Ephesus through house codes conveying a better life through mutual submission. Applying Paul's perspective to our marriage helped us to focus on submitting to each other, which increased our level of not only intimacy between us but also helped with blending our character and integrity. Such closeness helped with our love making as well.

Ephesians 5:21 describes the importance of submitting to one another out of reverence for Christ.

Marriage Lessons

Understanding the difference between sex and intimacy was very essential as related to our ability to connect physically. We recognized that we did not have an emotional connection which hindered the physical. It was more about connecting to fulfill our needs as a man and a woman. Although it was a challenge to become vulnerable enough with each other to develop a true emotional connection, we were able to eventually get to a good place.

Eventually, we began to focus on one another by spending more quality time, increasing the level of respect for one another, and focusing more on our emotional connection when we spent private time together. When we began to work harder to enhance our relationship, our intimacy moved beyond just sex, it was elevated to an emotional connection. We moved from being married with just physical chemistry to happily married with extreme passion and a deep emotional attachment to one another.

Marriage lessons on not honoring each other as king and queen. We realized our individual gifts brought new meaning to two flesh becoming one. We began to learn how to appreciate each other's individual gifts and focused on what the other brought to the marriage. We learned to understand that where one may have been weak, the other was strong, and that we complemented each other. The clarity of the significance of us complementing each other brought new meaning to us honoring each other as king and queen.

Marriage lessons on not making time for each other. Quality time is valuable time. When we started taking time for each other and appreciating our special time as a couple, we became closer. Valued time also helped us to realize that we needed time to recharge so that we would be less likely to take each other for granted. We learned to cherish our relationship and the sanctity of our marriage.

Marriage lessons on making love and spicing up the love life. Intimacy expands beyond sexual contact. Being emotionally and mentally connected with each other helped us to grow in our physical intimacy. Once we began to respect each other and honor the other as husband and wife, we truly became one.

Individuals may not agree with how we view our lessons in marriage. For us, they are a miracle because we lived the struggles, the hurt, and the pain. However, we respect the opinions of the naysayers. The biggest opposing view is that of individualism, which is more focused on self than team. For those who subscribe to this idea, you may be missing the bigger picture of the institution of marriage. Although a person has a right to have an individual identity, there is also a team identity composed by the family's name. In this space, one plus one equals one not two; the two become one flesh. The intimacy required here is a deep connection that goes beyond a single person. Therefore, there is value in honoring each other because you vowed to be together for a lifetime.

As a result, intimacy is one of the most desired parts of a marriage. Having the insight needed to treat each other as royalty, the king and the queen of your house, shows the importance of marriage, family, and exists as a legacy to your children. The ability to maintain the hard-earned gains in the marriage requires the same effort that it took to get there.

God showed us from our experiences how to apply
His leadership insights for lasting legacy.

Leadership Insights

God showed us from our experiences how to apply His leadership insights for lasting legacy. The patriarch, Abraham, demonstrated not only a sweet spot with his wife Sarah, he also walked in a place where God established him as the father of many nations. From his journey, we saw the making of a nation—his marriage to Sarah, his wife being desired by Egyptian kings, and his battle for his nephew. We also saw him blessed by king Melchizedek, the birth of Ishmael from Hagar, and their name change from Abram to Abraham and Sarai to Sarah. Furthermore, we saw his plea for Sodom and Gomorrah, the birth of Isaac from Sarah, Ishmael and Hagar leave, binding of Isaac, and the cave of the patriarchs (Gen. 11:27-25:10). We saw our mountain experience and intimate relationship between himself, Sarah, and God in Abraham's journey, specifically in Genesis 22:17-18, after he was willing to sacrifice his son from Sarah.

- I will bless you greatly
  - I will multiply your seed greatly
  - like the stars of the heavens
  - like the sand which is on the seashore.

- Your seed
  - will possess the gate of his enemies
  - will all the nations of the earth be blessed,
  - because you have obeyed my voice.

Abraham's and Sarah's journey and their intimate relation-ship with each other and God, strengthened us. Abraham loved his wife, his family, and his God, and went the extra mile. They were challenged on accounts with commitment and obedience, yet God's protection and blessings prevailed. He became the father of many nations, having influence lasting still today. As Abraham, we saw protection and blessings prevail in our marriage, allowing us to reach the level of love treating each other with honor, as king and queen. Looking forward, we are encouraged by Abraham's example that our legacy may be blessed also by our relationship with God.

Leadership insights on honoring each other as king and queen. Focusing on how to complement and cover each other is the key to honor. Such honor not only establishes intimacy between husband and wife, but also positions the marriage to be blessed by God.

Honoring your spouse can be hard but making the effort can be well worth it. Some practical ways that husbands can honor their wives are to serve her purpose, listen to her heart, engage her mind, protect her as a jewel, and love her as your queen. Likewise, here are some ways that wives can honor their husbands—letting him fail in God assists him in build a stronger relationship with God. God is the enforcer, treat your husband as the king, defend him, and focus on his strengths.

Leadership insights on making time for each other. Protecting the time that you spend with your spouse and your family is a wise investment. Such focused time can be used to bring members of the family together and identify and fix problems before they get worse.

Investing in your time is critical to understanding your family. This can be done in several ways. Establish family core values as a way to optimize time; block off time for the big things on the calendar right away; decide what your family is saying no to and stick to it; finally, making time for each other is sacred.

Leadership insights on making love and spicing up the love life. Connecting emotionally and mentally enhances physical intimacy. The deep connection is not only necessary to reaching the level of a successful marriage, it is also required when maintaining a healthy relationship.

Finding out how to connect emotionally can be fun and rewarding physically. To help with finding your reward, consider being emotionally available, put a fun list together, and conduct marriage enrichment activities. The bond strengthening of marriage will open up doors in the bedroom.

With life-changing insights gained, we are thrilled to see our love stronger than ever. However, we realize that some people approach spicing up their love life from the physical to emotional versus from the mind to the body as we did. These differences maybe minor, yet we realized physical love is good for the moment but does not last in the long run. The other perspective provides a place that holds while you are away from each other better.

With life-changing insights gained, we are thrilled to see our love stronger than ever.

In summary, it is important to understand that honoring your spouse leads to a deeper connection that aids with physical intimacy. Spending quality time also assists with maintaining a strong marriage. Having the insight to connect emotionally to God provides you the ability to position your family for generational blessings that money can't buy.

Conclusion

When couples fail to make love count towards intimacy such as the examples discussed in this chapter, their love may not reach the highest levels possible. From our discussions of honoring each other, ascending to the throne, making quality time last, and making love, we distilled how important recognizing the level of intimacy desired through connecting emotionally is in leading to a deeper physical connection. With our heart towards establishing the deep connection compared to only physical gratification, we learned that remaining in God's presence helped us to reach our marriage goals in His presence.

Not only did God provide the answer to our heart's cry, He gave us lessons in marriage through our experiences and insights with leadership found in His Word. Our marriage lessons helped us to treat each other as king and queen, establishing a model for our children to follow God's designed path. God's leadership insights illustrated what could happen by developing a deeper connection with Him and your spouse, as demonstrated through Abraham and Sarah. Such a deep connection is needed to sustain a long-lasting marriage. Next, we turn to the conclusion where we tie everything together. Before exploring Chapter 6, we have some thought provoking questions to help think about your level of intimacy in your marriage.

QUESTIONS FOR REFLECTION AND DISCUSSION

1. **Honoring each other as king and queen**—How have situations from the past limited your ability to honor each other as king and queen? What are some things that you have done to work on building genuine respect for one another? How are you willing to move forward in your marriage to build upon mutual respect between you and your spouse?

2. **Making time for each other**—Where are some of your favorite places to go as a couple? What are some of the things that you notice about your marriage when you spend quality time away with your spouse? What are some of your goals surrounding making time for each other?

3. **Making love and spicing up your love life**—How often do you relate intimacy to sex or physical contact? What are some things your spouse can do to build upon the emotional connection that enhances the physical intimacy? What are some things you feel your spouse needs to increase physical intimacy?

CONCLUSION

Throughout this book, we explored our experiences, our marriage lessons, our leadership insights using the Word of God and biblical scholarship. We hope our approach provides a tool for conversations and discussions that break down obstacles and barriers within your marriage. For those who are single, this work may provide a roadmap to God's plan for your marriage one day. Much like our roller coaster ride with having different viewpoints, respecting each other, building effective communication, resolving conflict, and developing intimacy, our journey has been well worth the effort. We are an ordinary married couple who put in the hard work and our trust in God, becoming a power couple through His grace and mercy. We believe that anyone can achieve the same status as a power couple with the right mindset and work ethic. We were driven to transform ourselves and our family, establishing a legacy for our children and grandchildren. As the reader, you may not always like our story or our how we treated each other, but our lessons and leadership insights merit some attention.

We decided to conclude our book with a brief summary. Combining all of our problems, our lessons, and our insights from the five chapters in one place, illustrates the broader picture. Through our detailed experiences, we hope you will use them by modifying, adjusting, and adapting our experiences to your relationship. By maximizing these lessons, insights, and questions at the end of the chapter, we hope you will be in a better position to improve your marriage or become better informed about God's design for marriage. To aid with remembering these hard-earned nuggets of wisdom, we offer some marriage and leadership maxims at the end of this book. These maxims are viewed as short, pithy statements expressing our truth from our experiences which are powerful and insightful to us. With that said, we turn to the combined sections from the book.

. . . we hope you will be in a better position to improve your marriage or become better informed about God's design for marriage.

Our Combined Problems and God's Combined Answers

In each chapter, our problems were distilled from our experiences. As we described our experiences, hopefully you clearly understood the significance of our highlighted problems. Furthermore, we wanted you to see yourself in our challenges to be better positioned and equipped to deal with similar problems in the future. We turned to God's Word for answers and the journey continued. We learned from some of God's best leaders like, Apostle Paul, Apostle Peter, King David and King Solomon, and the Lord Jesus Christ. We extracted their time locked insights from days past, we applied them to our problems, as follows.

In Chapter 1, we encountered problems with different viewpoints, miscommunication, and money as described in our upbringing, dating, and the early years of marriage. To deal with these problems, the Word of God urged us to shift our mindsets to Him to see the opportunities versus the problems that we faced. Problems with value, faith, love and respect, came along with avoiding divorce in Chapter 2. We fought for our marriage, gaining strength in God, transforming ourselves into victors in Christ instead of victims of life. Chapter 3 detailed our lack of success with non-verbal communication as problems with identifying the non-verbal, respecting each other's feelings, and building effective communication were highlighted. In our season of rest, the Word of God challenged us to stop being petty; we started loving each other which required listening.

Interestingly, Chapter 4 highlighted that we when did not listen and conflict occurred. The lack of attention resulted in problems with unhealthy ways to deal with conflict, healthy conflict resolution, and understanding love languages. Facing our inability to stay properly balanced and our inability to manage our obligations, the Holy Spirit illuminated ways for us the put our family first and find happiness God's way. Our lack of intimacy caused us to have problems with honoring each other as king and queen, making time for each other, making love, and spicing up our love life, as detailed in Chapter 5. Once we did the hard work, God quickly transitioned us from room-mates to honoring each other as king and queen.

Reflectively, as we look back at our problems,
it was clear that God matured us.

Reflectively, as we look back at our problems, it was clear that God matured us. He prepared us to not only face our problems, but also to have the resolve to search His Word for the answers and trust Him. Once we applied these principles to our marriage, they worked. Through seeking understanding from the scriptures, we learned some powerful marriage lessons that are noteworthy to review.

Combined Marriage Lessons

Every chapter has a marriage lesson section. We walked through the scriptures and explored the messages from God's leaders. We painted the picture based on the leader's such as Paul's context to show some of the linkages from their messages to our problems. We found similarities and differences, either way the dialogue with the God's text was interactive; we found ourselves facing some of the same problems and learning some of the same lessons, as detailed below.

We learned in Chapter 1 that overcoming unrealistic expectations took mutual agreement and honor, which was critical to being on one accord and aided in modeling a behavior for others. It was highlighted in Chapter 2 that God was the key focal point for valuing our spouse and becoming unified; this also assisted with preventing divorce. In Chapter 3, we noted that understanding your spouse's non-verbal cues was key to establishing open lines of communication. Chapter 4 included description of how we dealt with conflict and how learning the keys to building deep trust was understanding your spouse's love language. Last, we detailed in Chapter 5 that making love count and goes beyond the physical connection—dealing with mind and soul.

In sum, these lessons highlighted a process that took over 20 years. First, we built a bridge of trust that developed into bridge of mortar and brick connected to a castle where we honored each other as king and queen. Our castle was made of hard work that overcame hurt and pain, but our home is now a palace, of which we are proud. We are humbled by our journey and the path we have forged for our kids to review our lessons from leadership.

Combined Leadership Insights

In the leadership insights section, we turned to God for leadership insights to our problems. Beyond searching the scripture for leaders, we found something more. We discovered that our problems were not new; God had seen them before. With this revelation, we were excited to apply these insights to our lives and share them with you as summarized.

Chapter 1 unveiled God's plan for marriage in Genesis 2:24 that helped us to see His plan worked when we followed the blueprint and learned to submit our wills to God's. As we reflected on Chapter 2, we learned to trust God with our lives. King David also taught us that fighting, seeking and pursuing God helped with our building block of faith as we moved towards greater things. In Chapter 3, Adam showed us what not to do through his lack of communication with Eve, underscoring the importance to break through the noise to hear your spouse clearly. Apostle Paul urged us that it was possible to defend yourself in Chapter 4, highlighting that God's track record in our life provided us with ability to deal with conflict. In Chapter 5, Abraham and Sarah showed us how to have an intimate relationship with our spouse and a deeper connection with God that may lead to a generational blessing.

---

*. . . unpacking these century old leadership insights
helped us to become stronger leaders.*

Hence, unpacking these century old leadership insights helped us to become stronger leaders. These practical insights assisted us with breaking through the barriers between us in our marriage. Simply put, we were missing the mark and missed out on several good years in our marriage. However, with these insights firmly in hand, we are on the right path to make the most of the life we have left together.

Conclusion

While writing this book, we were able to identify things we can do to improve our marriage. There were things that we needed to do to improve our communication, enhancing our intimacy. We are firm believers that you never stop learning, and as we shared our experiences, not only were we able to recognize how much we have grown, but it gave also us something to look forward to as we continue to grow in strength and love. We truly understand that marriage is not easy, and that it takes work, but we are in it for the long haul. We give God all of the glory for where we are in our marriage because he has made us into a power couple, rooted and grounded in Him.

Unfortunately, our path to happiness may not work for you and some couples may have a different journey. For instance, we built our marriage on faith, whereas some couples don't have that common thread or even desire it. We used the team approach to marriage; others may use an individual mindset. We became one, compared to staying two. These comparisons illustrated the difference between God's and man's plan for marriage. This point suggests that following a proven blueprint is better than trying something new. Therefore, we recommend giving God's design for your marriage a try.

We hope this work blessed you! In addition, we have some resources in the back of the book that may provide additional insight for those who may be interested. Our goal is to assist those who may want to give their lives to Christ and try a different approach with their marriage. We also have the prayer of salvation with next steps for them located in the back. Furthermore, there is a sample prayer for couples that might want to start incorporating prayer in their marriage. Last, as mentioned before, we have some short reminders of nuggets gained from our experiences. We love you and hope you enjoy your journey as much as we have enjoyed ours. Our journey truly has been the good, the bad, and the ugly; but we thank God that we made it and so can you!

REFERENCES

Centers for Disease Control and Prevention (CDC). (2019). *Preventing intimate partner violence.* Retrieved from https://www.cdc.gov/violenceprevention/intimatepartnerviolence/fastfact.html

Chapman, G. (2015). *The 5 love languages: the secret to love that lasts.* Chicago, IL: Northfield Publishing.

Divorce rate by country: The world's 10 most and least divorced nations. (2020). Retrieved from https://www.unifiedlawyers.com.au/blog/global-divorce-rates-statistics/

Stritof, S. (2020). *What marital sex statistics can reveal.* Retrieved from https://www.verywellmind.com/what-marital-sex-statistics-can-reveal-2300946

U.S. Census Bureau. (2020, February 20). *How state marriage and divorce rates stack up.* Retrieved from https://www.census.gov/library/stories/2020/02/how-state-marriage-and-divorce-rates-stack-up.html

Yaffe, P. (2011). The 7% rule fact, fiction, or misunderstanding. *Ubiquity,* 2011, 1-5. doi:10.1145/2043155.2043156

ABOUT THE AUTHORS

SAMUEL L. HAYES, Jr., PhD, was born in Orlando, FL, and grew up abroad: Panama, Germany, Alaska, and NC. His family resides in the historic town of Fayetteville, North Carolina. He is the son of SFC (Ret.) Samuel and Marcia Hayes. Samuel adores his wife, Andrea, and their three adventurous children. Sam is a soldier, a clergyman, an academic, and a businessman. He combines scholarly insights with relevant experience to develop the next generation of strategic leaders.

Dr. Sam began his academic journey at Fayetteville State University and after enlisting in the U.S. Army, transitioned to the University of Phoenix where he graduated with a Bachelor's degree in Business Management. He continued his education, receiving a Master's in Business Administration (MBA) from American Intercontinental University, Master's in Information Strategy and Political Warfare from the Naval Postgraduate

School. He earned a Doctor of Philosophy (PhD) in Organization and Management with a Leadership specialization from Capella University and is pursuing a degree from Fuller Theological Seminary.

U.S. Army Major Hayes served as a Military Intelligence enlisted solider, and as a Cavalry officer. Currently, he is serving in special operations as a Civil Affairs officer with over 22 years of combined experience. Sam is the Apostle of His Glory International Ministries, an impactful author, and the CEO of Men of Distinction Excellence and Legacy (M.O.D.E.L.) a mentorship group for young men. Sam is a member of Kappa Alpha Psi Fraternity, Inc.

To reach Sam for information on leadership, strategic design, consulting, or guest speaking please visit his **websites: drsam-drdreahayes.com** or **e-mail: drsamhayesjr@gmail.com**

ANDREA HAYES, PhD, LCMHC was raised in St. Pauls, NC, but was born in Miami, FL. She is the daughter of Albert and Rosie Marsh, Sr. She is a devoted wife to Samuel L. Hayes, Jr., and the proud mother of three beautiful children (Stefone, Shirod, and Ashara); her love for her family is indescribable. She is a former educator who is now a therapist. Her passion for helping people is the driving force behind her determination to make a difference within her local community and the Christian community, nationally and internationally.

Andrea is a proud graduate of Fayetteville State University with a bachelor's degree in English Literature. After undergraduate school, she continued her education and became a licensed middle grades educator. The passion that she has for helping students led her to eventually become a Licensed Clinical Mental Health Counselor (LCMHC) and earn her PhD in Advanced Studies in Human Behavior (Counseling).

Andrea is also the Prophetess of His Glory International Ministries. She is an up and coming author, the Founder / CEO of Rivers of Peace Counseling Services, PLLC, and the founder Ladies of Vivid Elegance (L.O.V.E.), a mentorship group for young ladies. She is also a member of Delta Sigma Theta Sorority, Inc.

To reach Andrea for counseling, consulting, or motivational speaking engagements, please visit her **websites: drsam-drdrea-hayes.com** or **e-mail: drdreahayes@gmail.com**

THE PRAYER OF SALVATION

If you declare with your mouth, "Jesus is Lord," and believe in your heart that God raised him from the dead, you will be saved. For it is with your heart that you believe and are justified, and it is with your mouth that you profess your faith and are saved (Rom. 10:9-10).

Dear Lord Jesus,

    Thank you for dying on the cross for my sin. Please forgive me. Come into my life. I receive You as my Lord and Savior. Now, help me to live for you the rest of this life.

In the name of Jesus, I pray.

Amen

NOW WHAT?

If you just prayed a sincere prayer of faith and you're wondering what to do next as a new Christian, check out these helpful suggestions:

- Salvation is by grace, and through faith. There is nothing you did, or ever can do, to deserve it. Salvation is a free gift from God. All you have to do is receive it.

- Tell someone about your decision. Find a brother or sister in the Lord and tell him or her, "Hey, I made a decision to follow Jesus." It is a great way to celebrate.

- Talk to God every day. Build a relationship with Him and be yourself. Thank the Lord daily for salvation. Pray for others in need. Seek His direction. Pray for the Lord to fill you with His Holy Spirit. There is no limit to prayer. You can pray with your eyes closed or open, while sitting or standing, kneeling or lying on your bed, anywhere, anytime.

- Find a church and get plugged in somewhere.

MARRIED COUPLE'S PRAYER

Dear Heavenly Father,

Thank you for blessing us to find each other and to grow more in love with each other, but most of all, more in love with you. Lord, thank you for keeping us and leading us on the path for righteousness for Your name's sake (Ps. 23:2). We are grateful that you have kept us thus far and praise your name for continuing to keep us in years to come.

Lord, let your fire cover and protect us (Exod. 14:24) from anyone or anything that tries to come against our marriage. Lord, continue to load us with your benefits (Ps. 68:19) as we grow stronger in you. Lord, you said in your word, the tongue is but a small member, but it is powerful (James 3:5). We speak blessings over our lives and over our marriage. Lord, we pray that you will let us grow in grace and in the knowledge of Jesus Christ. Thank you Lord for allowing us to be a blessing to others and an example of what a wonderful, prosperous marriage should be.

Lord, we praise you for in thee, our family is blessed (Gen. 12:3). We come against any generational curses that try to attach themselves to us or our children, in Jesus' name. Lord, please, allow your fire to be released and let the works of darkness be cast into deep pits, that they will not rise up again (Ps. 140:10). Lord, we give you glory for everything that you have done for us. Thank you for your grace, mercy and love. In Jesus' name we pray. Thank God.

Amen

DR. SAM'S &
DR. DREA'S MAXIMS

FOR MAKING LOVE WORK

*By not honoring your mutual agreements, you are weakening
your marriage rather than forging a future together.*

* * *

*Defending your marriage from outside influences,
strengthens the bond between you, your spouse, and God.*

* * *

*If you aren't passionate about understanding how
your spouse communicates, don't be surprised
by the marriage dying around you.*

* * *

*Resolving conflict with love is a choice,
and your spouse knows the difference.*

* * *

If you won't get close, you will never experience intimacy.

FOR LEADING YOUR FAMILY

If you are not leveraging God's blueprint, you are using an inadequate roadmap rather than leading your family towards success.

* * *

If you are not fighting alongside your spouse, you will eventually start to fight against them or worst, fighting alone.

* * *

Cutting through the noise and clutter is not always easy, but being aligned with your spouse and God clears the path for the souls to communicate.

* * *

Sometimes conflict is the only way forward; enjoy the journey to a better you and a stronger marriage.

* * *

Honoring your spouse is a choice, your love life will know the difference.

INDEX

www.ingramcontent.com/pod-product-compliance
Lightning Source LLC
Chambersburg PA
CBHW050733030426

42336CB00012B/1537